Peredur

Peredur

The Undiscovered Truth of the Nazi Grail Quest

David James Senior

Pen & Sword
MILITARY

First published in Great Britain in 2024 by
Pen & Sword Military
An imprint of Pen & Sword Books Limited
Yorkshire – Philadelphia

ISBN 978 1 03611 051 2

A CIP catalogue record for this book is available from the British Library

Typeset by Mac Style
Printed in the UK by CPI Group (UK) Ltd, Croydon, CR0 4YY.

MIX
Paper | Supporting responsible forestry
FSC® C013604
FSC www.fsc.org

Pen & Sword Books Limited incorporates the imprints of After the Battle, Atlas, Archaeology, Aviation, Discovery, Family History, Fiction, History, Maritime, Military, Military Classics, Politics, Select, Transport, True Crime, Air World, Frontline Publishing, Leo Cooper, Remember When, Seaforth Publishing, The Praetorian Press, Wharncliffe Local History, Wharncliffe Transport, Wharncliffe True Crime and White Owl.

For a complete list of Pen & Sword titles please contact

PEN & SWORD BOOKS LIMITED
47 Church Street, Barnsley, South Yorkshire, S70 2AS, England
E-mail: enquiries@pen-and-sword.co.uk
Website: www.pen-and-sword.co.uk
or
PEN AND SWORD BOOKS
1950 Lawrence Road, Havertown, PA 19083, USA
E-mail: uspen-and-sword@casematepublishers.com
Website: www.penandswordbooks.com

Contents

Part I

The Nazi Quest for the Holy Grail

'As I stand before the Devil's stone, as I touch it and as I see it gently lit up by the stars – which, in the sky, follow imperturbably their divine path –, so too I think of the Grail.'[1]

SS Obersturmführer Otto Rahn (c.1937)

Prologue to Part I

'No dream is too big or unattainable under the Nazis.'[1]

These were the words of Otto Rahn, after delivering a lecture detailing his quest to find the Holy Grail, to a captivated audience made up of members of the German Ancestral Heritage Research and Teaching Society, or Deutches Ahnenerbe, a Nazi think tank founded by Heinrich Himmler.

The role of the Ahnenerbe was to rediscover the achievements of the so-called Aryan race in ancient times and bring them to the attention of the German public. A branch of the SS, its members, dressed in the black ceremonial uniform of the regiment, complete with daggers and other SS trimmings were scholars and intellectuals attracted to the Nazi ideal.

Lest it be thought the Ahnenerbe was a benign organisation of academics, scientists in the Ahnenerbe, with no regard for humanity, performed numerous horrific experiments on Jewish prisoners, including ones to try and determine antidotes for mustard gas and malaria, exposing prisoners to an excruciating death.

By the time he delivered his lecture to the Ahnenerbe, Rahn had become a leading Nazi, with the distinguished rank of Obersturmführer SS, having been admitted to the Black Order or Allgemeine-SS (a prestigious non-combatant branch of the SS) on 12 March 1936 on the personal instruction of Himmler.

Chapter 1

The Early Life of Otto Rahn

According to a document he wrote in support of his entry to the SS, Otto Wilhelm Rahn was born on 18 February 1904, in Michelstadt, Odenwald, Germany. His parents were Karl and Clara Rahn. His father, Karl, was a civil servant. He was raised in a 'run of the mill', middle-class home, by parents who held conformist Protestant Christian beliefs. An unremarkable beginning to what would ultimately prove to be a very remarkable life.

With geography playing its part, it was in these formative years that the seeds of Rahn's fascination with the Grail were sown. Some 20km east of his birthplace in Michelstadt stands Wildenberg Castle referred to by Rahn as the 'Grail Castle' because it was here that Wolfram von Eschenbach had written *Parzival*, which is the Arthurian tale of a knight's quest to become 'Lord of the Grail'. As Rahn later put it 'I am therefore come from a world in orbit of the Grail.'[1]

Rahn's adoring mother kindled a love of literature in her young son. She fired his imagination with tales of King Arthur and the Knights of the Round Table, but it was the tale of Parzival and his quest for the Grail, that Rahn cherished most.

In 1910, aged 6, Rahn entered junior school, where, by his own admission, he spent much of his time looking out of the window daydreaming, his mind being preoccupied with tales of antiquity.

There is some evidence to suggest that during his school years Rahn was a member of the Wandervogel, a German youth movement formed in 1901, promoting freedom, self-reliance and a spirit of adventure among its members, a movement akin to the boy scouts. It is likely that, while a member of this movement, Rahn acquired a taste for the type of expeditions he would later mount in search of the Grail.

The Wandervogel on expedition in Germany.

Despite his daydreaming, Rahn left school having achieved his baccalaureate in 1924 and enrolled in law studies, first at Freiburg then at Heidelberg. On completing these studies, he commenced a doctorate, specialising in the literary history of the languages and romances of southern France and, remembering his childhood hero, Parzival, he took for his thesis 'The Research of Master Kyot of Wolfram von Eschenbach', which he dedicated to the author of *Parzival*, to Wagner and the 'troubadours' in 1929. His nod to the composer Wagner is an acknowledgement of the contribution made by Wagner to the legend of Parzival by writing, to great acclaim, a tributary opera entitled *Parsifal*.

At this time, however, Rahn lacked the dedication he later showed in his quest for the Grail and failed to complete his doctorate, choosing instead to embark upon a period of travelling, taking in various parts of France, Switzerland, Spain and Italy. Furthermore, Rahn was rather scrawny and sickly in appearance, and somewhat of a bookworm in nature.

All the same, he would eventually become the adventurer and relic hunter whose exploits were the historical inspiration for the movie escapades of the fictional swashbuckler and archaeologist 'Indiana Jones', famously played by Harrison Ford. Paradoxically, Rahn would be searching for the Nazis, rather than competing against them as Jones did in *Indiana Jones and the Last Crusade*. Overleaf, Indiana Jones in his trademark fedora on the left, while Otto Rahn in his on the right.

Promotional poster showing Indiana Jones donned in a Fedora hat.

Otto Rahn similarly attired.

Chapter 2

Rahn's Quest for the Holy Grail Commences

It was whilst on his travels to parts of western Europe that Rahn determined to improve his level of health and physical fitness through a daily regime of skiing. At the same time, Rahn became inspired by the work of the German archaeologist Heinrich Schliemann, who by searching for geographical clues in Homer's *Iliad* had located the lost city of Troy in 1873. Seeking adventure, the invigorated Rahn figured that by carrying out a similar analysis of the legend of Parzival, his childhood hero, who according to legend had sought and found the Grail, he would find clues that would lead him to the whereabouts of the Holy Grail.

Through knowledge he had picked up on his travels, talking to locals and trawling through library books, as well as conversations he had with fellow intellectuals, Rahn deduced that the place where, according to legend, Parzival discovered the Grail, Munsalvaeche, was in fact the ancient fortress of Montségur in the mountains of south-west France.

This was based on his belief that the Cathars, a thirteenth-century religious sect predominantly based in the south-west of France were the basis for Wolfram von Eschenbach's 'Grail Knights', keepers of the Grail at the Grail Castle of Munsalvaeche.

The fortress at Montségur was the last bastion of the Cathars, who Rahn believed were the true 'Grail Knights'. Therefore, it followed that Montségur, their fortress, was the site of 'Munsalvaeche' the 'Grail Castle'. It then figured that Montségur would be where he would find the Grail.

Perhaps most influential, of the people he spoke to, was Antonin Gadal, who he met in the French town of Ussat-les-Bains. Gadal was a member of the Friends of Montségur and the Grail, a society that believed there was a link between the Cathars and the Grail.

Rahn had briefly considered the role played by the Templar Knights with respect to the Grail and the Grail romances. But conversations he had with Gadal, led him to believe that the Cathars, considered heretics by the Catholic church, were the real Grail Knights, keepers of the Grail, in the legend of Parzival.

Rahn felt an affinity with the Cathars; he claimed they had been first brought to his attention whilst at junior school by his religious studies tutor, Baron von Gall. The affinity he felt with them was perhaps borne of him being somewhat of an outsider, having empathy for a persecuted minority.

In 1931, following up on his belief that the Cathars were the true 'Grail Knights', Rahn made his way to the Languedoc region of France, where Montségur, their fortress, lay, and so began his quest to find the Grail. Posing as a journalist, he interviewed locals to gain further clues as to the whereabouts of the Grail, delving into local legends suggesting his initial instincts were correct and the Grail was waiting somewhere in the foothills of the nearby Pyrenees, for him to discover.

Rahn scoured passages of Eschenbach's *Parzival* seeking out further clues. He quoted the passage below as evidence that the Grail lay hidden in a cave, concealed in the limestone cliffs upon which the Cathar fortress was built:

> *'His host led Parsifal into the grotto*
> *Well protected from the wind…*
> *There was a coat lying there*
> *The hermit lent it him to put on*
> *And then took him to another grotto'*[1]

The prospect of him finding perhaps the greatest treasure known to man, which had lay hidden for almost 1,000 years, drew Rahn into an obsessive search, in which he meticulously combed the caves lying beneath the hills of Montségur.

Rahn, the action man, scouring the caves lying beneath the hills of Montségur.

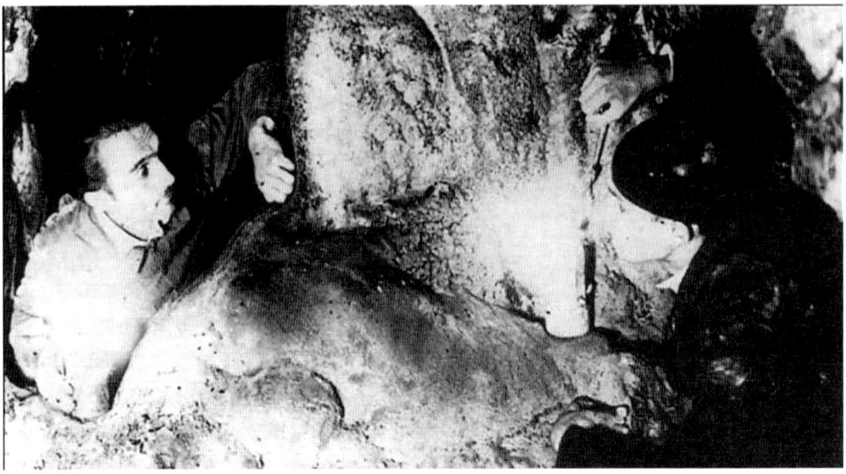

Rahn in the Cave of the Hermit, 1932.

Convinced that it was only a matter of time before he found the Grail but frustrated that a lack of finance had curtailed his search, Rahn wrote a book *Crusade Against the Grail* in which he detailed his findings, in the hope of securing enough funds to bring his search to fruition. The first edition of this work appeared on the streets of Germany in 1933.

Chapter 3

Hitler, Wagner and *Parsifal*

Rahn's admiration of Wagner and of his last work, *Parsifal*, evidenced by the dedication he made to Wagner in producing his doctoral thesis, was shared by none other than Adolf Hitler. When Hitler wrote *Mein Kampf* in 1924, he felt moved to say 'I attended a performance of *Lohengrin*, the first opera I had ever heard. I was fascinated at once.'[1] *Lohengrin*, a prequel to *Parsifal*, was the first fruit of Wagner's fascination with the Holy Grail myths of Arthurian legend. The end point of this fascination would be his final masterpiece *Parsifal*; the opera described by Wagner's widow, Cosima as his 'last card'. *Parsifal* opens in the forest near the castle of the Brotherhood of the Grail and climaxes with the title character becoming king, and the reunion of the Holy Grail with the Holy Spear, saving the brotherhood.

Both the Holy Spear and the Holy Grail in Wagner's opera *Parsifal* possessed magical properties. The Holy Spear being representative of the spear that pierced the side of Christ at the crucifixion, and the Holy Grail being the cup with which Christ commanded the disciples to drink his blood at the Last Supper.

The cup used by Christ at the Last Supper, subsequently referred to outside of the Bible as the Holy Grail is referenced in the book of Matthew:

> *'And he took the cup, and gave thanks, and gave it to them, saying, Drink ye all of it;*
> *For this is my blood of the new testament, which is shed for many for the remission of sins.*

But I say unto you, I will not drink henceforth of this fruit of the vine, until that day when I drink it new with you in my Father's kingdom.'

Matthew 26:27–29 (KJV)

The spear that pierced Christ's side at the crucifixion, subsequently referred to in Wagner's *Parsifal* as the Holy Spear, is referenced in the book of John:

'The Jews, therefore, because it was the preparation, that the bodies should not remain upon the cross on the sabbath day, (for that sabbath day was a high day,) besought Pilate that their legs might be broken, and that they might be taken away.

Then came the soldiers, and break the legs of the first, and of the other which was crucified with him.

But when they came to Jesus, and saw that he was dead already, they break not his legs:

But one of the soldiers with a spear pierced his side, and forthwith came there out blood and water.

And he that saw it bare record, and his record is true: and he knoweth that he saith true, that ye might believe.

For these things were done, that the scripture should be fulfilled, a bone of him shall not be broken.

And again, another scripture saith, they shall look on him whom they pierced.

And after this Joseph of Arimathea, being a disciple of Jesus, but secretly for fear of the Jews, besought Pilate that he might take away the body of Jesus: and Pilate gave him leave. He came therefore and took the body of Jesus.'

John 19:31–38 (KJV)

According to some Grail legends, the Last Supper cup dubbed the Holy Grail was also the cup used by Joseph of Arimathea to catch the blood of Christ dripping from the lance wound he received.

Both these objects would be hunted by the Nazis as prized relics to be displayed in their 'Grail Castle' yet to be built. This would be the fulfilment of Hitler's ambition to emulate the feats of Parsifal in reuniting the spear with the Grail.

Wagner and his 'Grail' operas became an obsession of Hitler. When Hitler left his hometown of Linz to live in Vienna in 1905, aged 18, he found solace in passing his time away at the opera. It was here that his passion for *Parsifal* was ignited. Whist in Vienna, Hitler would also have taken time to marvel at the Holy Spear, which at that time was preserved in Vienna along with other relics of the Holy Roman Empire, collectively known as the Imperial Regalia. It wasn't until 1913 that Hitler moved from Vienna to Munich, and by this time, his passion for Wagner and in particular *Parsifal* had developed into a lifelong obsession.

This obsession and the close relationship Hitler enjoyed with Wagner's family are demonstrated by what happened at the Bayreuth Festspielhaus, an opera house built in 1873 by Wagner, solely dedicated to the performance of his works.

By the time the Nazis came to power in 1933, the original sets at the Bayreuth Festspielhaus were still being used and were badly in need of replacement. In the normal course of events, this work would have been overseen by Emil Preetorius, who had become the director of the Bayreuth Festival, the annual celebration of Wagner's operas, performed at the Festspielhaus. However, a petition was launched and when over 1,000 signatures had been collected it was sent by Winifred Wagner, the English born wife of Siegfried Wagner, the son of the great master, to Hitler, along with a pamphlet proclaiming Preetorius as 'un-German' and 'under Jewish influence'. Preetorius mixed with a precarious circle of friends, including Thomas Mann, a supporter of liberal democracy in Germany, who emigrated to Switzerland when the Nazis came to power. Without hesitation, Hitler appointed Alfred Roller, an artist and set designer he had become acquainted with when he was an aspiring artist, in Preetorius's place. Roller produced sets

A painting by Theodor Pixis of the set design for the original 1882 production of *Parsifal.*

very much in keeping with the originals. However, the temple of the Grail had lost its cupola, and this displeased the conservative faction of the opera community. A further appeal by Winifred to Hitler resulted in Wieland Wagner, Winifred's son, being given responsibility for redesigning the sets. Unsurprisingly, what Wieland produced in 1937 was retrograde and completely in line with the traditional preferences of Hitler.

In a similar vein, Hitler was so impressed by Franz Stassen's collection of fifteen *Parsifal* illustrations that he commissioned Stassen to create four tapestries for the Reich Chancellery. Stassen was an illustrator who had studied at the Berlin College of Fine Arts between 1896 and 1892. In 1930, Stassen joined the NDSAP, a forerunner of the Nazi Party, and his work made such an impression on Hitler that in 1939 he awarded Stassen the title of professor. In the dying throes of the Second World War, Hitler named Stassen on the Gottbegnadeten list

Scenes from Alfred Roller's set designs for the 1934 production of *Parsifal*.

Scenes from Wieland Wagner for the 1937 production with the cupola restored for the later scenes.

(an inventory of artists considered crucial to National Socialist culture) as a 'divine blessed' fine artist in recognition of his contribution to the Nazi regime.

Hitler attended the Bayreuth Festival featuring *Parsifal* every summer from 1933 to 1939.

When Hitler visited Wagner's villa in Bayreuth, he was greeted enthusiastically by the composer's widow, Cosima, son, Siegfried, and daughter-in-law, Winifred. Winifred later recalled that Hitler 'visited the master's grave alone, and came back in a state of great emotion, saying "Out of *Parsifal* I make a religion."'[2]

Hitler elaborated on his thoughts about *Parsifal* when he wrote *Mein Kampf*: 'What is celebrated is not the Christian religion of compassion, but pure and noble blood, blood whose purity the brotherhood of initiates has come together to guard. Wagner's line of thought is intimately familiar to me.' Hitler once said, 'At every stage of my life I come back to him.'[3]

Franz Stassen's illustration of *Parsifal*, Act 3, Scene 2, with the Grail and the spear reunited.

Parsifal Revealing the Holy Grail, Franz Stassen's illustration for the end of Act 3. Parsifal raises the Grail in blessing of the knighthood, as a white dove descends and hovers above him.

Hitler refers here to a view of Christianity set out in an article written by Wagner, 'Heroism and Christianity', and printed in the journal *Bayreuth Blatter* in 1881. Sadly, the article amounts to little more than a racist rant.

Hitler's absolute obsession with all things related to Wagner and *Parsifal* is further illustrated by the way he decorated his private quarters. In 1935, Hitler decided to redecorate his spacious Munich apartment at a cost of 120,000 reichsmarks, an amount more than ten times the average salary of a German doctor that year. A contemporary report in *The Daily Telegraph* stated that:

> *'all the furnishings and decorations are being carried out to Herr Hitler's own designs' then went on to detail Hitler's love for German art and his passion for music before saying 'the decorations in his flat follow the German heroic colour scheme of blue, gold and white, made famous by Wagner's operas, and the furnishing is all of the same style. This mirrors the design of the throne room at the residence of King Ludwig II of Bavaria.'*[14]

All this is testament to Hitler's lifelong obsession with *Parsifal.*

Adolf Hitler and Winfred Wagner together before the performance of *Parsifal* in the Festspielhaus, 1935.

Hitler walks the grounds of the Festspielhaus with Winifred Wagner and her children, Wieland and Wolfgang, in 1937.

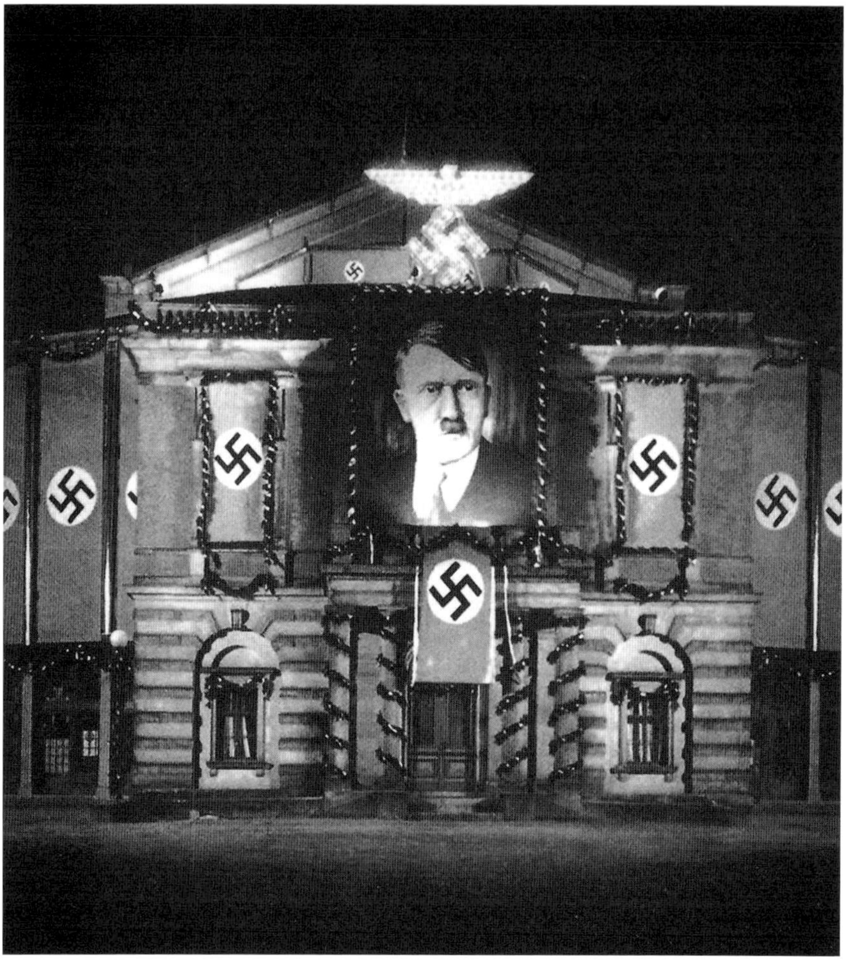

The Festspielhaus decorated and illuminated to celebrate Hitler's birthday on 20 April 1939.

Chapter 4

Ludwig II

It could well be that Hitler's traditional views on the depiction of the story of Parsifal were inspired, or perhaps reinforced, by King Ludwig II of Bavaria. For much of his adult life, Hitler resided in Bavaria, either in Munich, the state capital, or at the Berghof, his Bavarian mountain retreat. Ludwig was described by a contemporary political commentator as the 'only true king of this century'. Ludwig was possessed by the idea of a holy kingdom bestowed upon him by the grace of God. A view it is not difficult to imagine Hitler empathising with. In reality, Ludwig was a constitutional monarch, a head of state with rights and duties and little freedom of action. As a reaction to this, he built a fantasy world around him; the 'New Castle' (Neuschwanstein) he built was based on Christian kingship in the Middle Ages.

Ludwig increasingly identified himself with Parzival, the legendary medieval figure who became Grail king. Neuschwanstein was reinterpreted as the castle of the Holy Grail. The murals in the Singers' Hall depict the Parzival Saga, those in the salon the Lohengrin Saga. The Throne Room was redesigned as the Hall of the Holy Grail – dedicated to the mystery of salvation for the world. Ludwig took the stage design for Wagner's *Parsifal* and personalised it. The room was transformed into a grand hall decorated with gold leaf, porphyry and lustrous blue and gold mosaics. A colour scheme remarkably like the one chosen by Hitler for the refurbishment of his apartment. Hitler knew Neuschwanstein well; this is evidenced by a painting he did of Neuschwanstein in 1914.

As a crown prince, Ludwig was already fascinated by the musical dramas and writings of Richard Wagner. In 1864, he summoned Wagner to meet him, and after the meeting, Wagner felt compelled to write:

> *'Today I was brought to him. He is unfortunately so beautiful and wise, soulful and lordly, that I* fear *his life must fade away like a divine dream in this base world … You cannot imagine the magic of his regard: if he remains alive it will be a great miracle!'*[1]

Wagner enjoyed lavish support from Ludwig, who provided finance for the building of Wagner's new opera house or festival theatre, the Bayreuth Festspielhaus, where *Parsifal* was premiered in 1882. An act replicated by Hitler when he responded to the pleas of Wagner's descendants regarding refurbishing the Festspielhaus. Without Ludwig II's commitment, the Bayreuth Festival, which Hitler attended every year from 1933 to 1939, would not have come into being. It is possible the admiration for Wagner by Ludwig was not entirely reciprocated because Wagner and his circle privately referred to Ludwig as 'Parsifal', and his problems were incorporated into the operatic drama of the Grail.

Ludwig's influence on Hitler is underlined in a passage he wrote in *Mein Kampf*:

> *'Even the great cities become more barren of real works of art the more they increase in population. They assume more and more a neutral atmosphere and present the same aspect, though on a larger scale, as the wretched little factory towns. Everything that our modern age has contributed to the civilisation of our great cities is absolutely deficient. All our towns are living on the glory and the treasures of the past. If we take away from the Munich of today everything that was created under Ludwig II, we should be horror-stricken to see how meagre has been the output of important artistic creations since that time.'*[2]

When Hitler was discharged from the army after the First World War in 1920, he lived in Munich, moving into his apartment there in 1929. Munich, the capital of the state of Bavaria, was the birthplace of the Nazi Party. Hitler, just like Ludwig before him, was a fantasist, who was trying to create a reality out of Germanic myth and the Grail legends of Parsifal and Lohengrin.

Design for Neuschwanstein Castle by Christian Jank in 1868, which incorporated Richard Wagner's instructions for the set of Act 2 of the opera *Lohengrin*.

Neuschwanstein Castle, as it stands today, in Bavaria.

Parzival at the Court of Amfortas, detail from the mural by August Spiess (1883/84) in the Singers' Hall, Neuschwanstein Castle.

Parzival fighting the Red Knight, mural by August Spiess (1883/84) in the Singers' Hall, Neuschwanstein Castle.

Painting of Neuschwanstein by Hitler, 1914.

Chapter 5

Enter the Nazis

The publication of Rahn's *Crusade Against the Grail* coincided with the Nazi's coming to power in Germany. The Nazis took office largely on the back of a pledge to restore national pride in Germany. The reparations paid by Germany under the terms of the Treaty of Versailles had left the nation economically crippled, and the depression that came with this left the country in desperate need of a lift. Hitler was a populist and promised to make the nation great again. The means by which this would be done were multi-faceted, and an aspect of this would be creating a heritage that the Germans could be proud of and a present that would provide a legacy for future generations. Finding the Holy Grail would make an impressive addition to the picture they were painting. Beyond this, there is a strong chance that Hitler believed by reuniting the Holy Spear with the Holy Grail he would secure the future of the Reich, just as *Parsifal* had secured the future of the Grail brotherhood.

Whilst he knew the whereabouts of the Holy Spear, the location of the Holy Grail remained a mystery. If he were to reconcile the Grail with the Spear, he would first have to find it.

It may well be that Hitler's first port of call in taking steps to realise this ambition was to try and secure the services of an established 'Grail hunter' already known to him, Walter Johannes Stein.

All we can say for certain in relation to this is that Walter Stein's time spent living in Vienna coincided with the time Hitler spent living in Vienna (1905–13). Stein was born in Vienna in 1891. He went on to study and then lecture at the University of Vienna, with his time there disrupted by service in the Austrian army during the First World War. Also, Stein left Germany for Britain in 1932.

However, we can make use here of testament provided by a certain Trevor Ravenscroft. To say that Ravenscroft is an interesting character would be an understatement. Ravenscroft served in the British special forces during the Second World War and was part of the reconnaissance party that, in October 1941, paved the way for the failed attempt by the Allies, codenamed Operation Flipper, to assassinate General Erwin Rommel in North Africa.

Ravenscroft is most famous though for writing *The Spear of Destiny*, a much-criticised study of occult powers of the spear, which is also known as the *Holy Spear*, as perceived by the Nazis and in particular Adolf Hitler.

In this work, Ravenscroft claims that through a shared interest in the mysteries of the Holy Grail and the Holy Lance or Spear, Stein came to know Adolf Hitler during the winter of 1912 when they were both resident in Vienna. He said Stein and Hitler engaged in a series of discussions throughout the winter of 1912 and the spring of 1913 concerning the mysteries of the Grail and the Spear. According to Ravenscroft, Stein 'watched at close quarters' Hitler's rise to power as leader of the Nazi Party. Furthermore, he alleges that Stein leaving Germany and coming to Britain was the direct result of Heinrich Himmler, who we shall hear much more of soon, trying to recruit Stein into the SS to carry out research into the occult and presumably hunt down the Grail on behalf of the Nazis.

Ravenscroft work, *The Spear of Destiny*, is largely written off by commentators as being a pseudohistory and, to a great extent, a work of fantasy. The principal allegation being that Ravenscroft never met Stein as he claims he did in the book. However, to disregard everything Ravenscroft says would be an error. We ignore 'pseudohistory' at our peril; it often contains more than a grain of truth, with the author filling in the gaps in their knowledge with reasoned supposition and perhaps some element of fantasy to spice up the story. Ravenscroft was well connected to sources in the army and British aristocracy, and he might well have had access to information not widely available to others.

Whether Stein was the Nazis first choice as Grail hunter or not we cannot be sure. Similarly, we know Stein had links with Winston Churchill and the British government. Whether these links were connected to his knowledge of the Holy Grail, and the Nazis wish to possess it, is open to conjecture.

Either way, not long after being published, Rahn's work came to the attention of Heinrich Himmler. Himmler was a key member of the Nazi inner circle, and in 1933, he was head of the Schutzstaffel or SS, Hitler's personal bodyguard. Himmler had moulded the SS to fit the chivalric ideals of their mythical Aryan forefathers.

Himmler was born and raised in Munich, the Bavarian capital, and his godfather was none other than Prince Heinrich of Bavaria. Each night before he and his brother Gebhardt went to bed as children, they were made to pray in front of an ivory statue of Christ on the cross. The significance of spiritual, particularly Christian, artefacts cannot have been lost on him.

As a 6-year-old, he took part in a family holiday to Füssen, barely a mile from Neuschwanstein Castle built by Ludwig II, an ancestor of Himmler's godfather. The young Himmler could not have failed to be influenced by the rich tapestry of German mythology and Grail legend he encountered there.

The Nazi inner circle, of which Himmler was a key member, was nothing like a tight-knit band of brothers. Hermann Göring, Joseph Goebbels, Rudolf Hess, Martin Bormann and others all vied for Hitler's attention and courted his favour. They were a treacherous bunch, who would think nothing of stabbing each other in the back for the sake of personal gain. This situation was not improved when, around this time, Ernst Rohm re-entered the inner circle having returned from exile in Bolivia. Rohm was one of Hitler's oldest allies, having taken part in the Munich Beer Hall Putsch, when the Nazis tried to seize power by force in 1923. On his return, Rohm was reinstated as head of the SA or brown shirts, the paramilitary arm of the Nazi Party and a rival organisation to the SS. Under Rohm's leadership, the SA ranks had swelled in number from a couple of hundred thousand to over 4 million men. The SA massively outnumbered Himmler's SS. Rohm had quickly become a threat to the ambitious Himmler, who was by now subordinate to Rohm and directly under his command. Himmler was an utterly repulsive character, insecure, sycophantic, ruthless, masochistic and manipulative. But Himmler was also resourceful, and when Rahn's *Crusade Against the Grail*, claiming that the Holy Grail was within touching distance of being found, came to his attention, this must have seemed like manna from heaven. Whether he had tried to recruit Stein into the SS for the purpose of hunting the Grail and been rebuffed or not, Himmler was gripped by Rahn's work immediately. The theories put forward by Rahn presented a chance for Himmler to capture the Grail and afford his master, Hitler, the opportunity of emulating the feats of his beloved Parsifal.

This would be a real coup for the Nazis and surely earn Himmler the undying gratitude of the Führer. Without hesitation, Himmler summoned Rahn and offered him 1,000 reichsmarks a month to continue his search for the Grail on condition that he joined the SS. This equates to an annual salary of around £90,000 in 2024. Rahn accepted the offer. Himmler's vision of recreating a mythical Aryan past of a holy order of knights was beginning to come together.

Chapter 6

Wewelsburg Castle

A key part of the mythical past the Nazis were creating would be the establishment of a citadel, a sacred fortress, that could be used by the elite brotherhood of the Nazis for ceremonial purposes, such as swearing in 'knights' of the SS.

In 1933, the same year Rahn's work was published, Himmler first visited Wewelsburg Castle. At the time, the castle was derelict and neglected. Himmler commissioned an order for the castle to be to be lent and made plans for alterations to the structure to be made. This was to be the Nazis 'Neuschwanstein', their version of the 'Grail Castle' or 'Camelot'. A place where senior SS officers could stay and immerse themselves in legends of the fatherland.

A year later, a contract was made for the SS to lease the castle from the district of Buren for the period of 100 years at a cost of one reichsmark per year.

Initially, the reconstruction of the castle was paid for by a combination of funding from the Prussian state, the Nazi Party and private benefactors. To escape financial supervision by the state and the Nazi Party, Himmler and six other SS officers founded the 'Registered Charity for the Promotion and Care of German Cultural Monuments'. This newly formed organisation became incorporated into the SS and supervised the building work at Wewelsburg. The new arrangement gave Himmler a free hand to let his imagination run riot. Himmler would replicate what Ludwig II had done with Neuschwanstein, casting the SS as the brotherhood of Grail knights central to Wagner's operas. 'Never forget,' Himmler told a gathering of SS officers 'we are a knightly Order, from which we cannot withdraw, to which one is recruited by blood and within which one remains with body and soul so long as one lives on this earth.'[1] Wewelsburg was to be their citadel. When war broke out in 1939, Wewelsburg became a meeting place for the SS generals.

In 1940, a new concentration camp was built 600m from the castle to house inmates who would provide slave labour to carry out the building work desired by the Nazis.

Building work took place at Wewelsburg right up until 1945. By this time, the castle was everything Himmler had imagined it would be. A dark, eerily echoing, vaulted crypt with twelve pedestals around the wall, and a gas pipe for an eternal flame in the centre was created at the base of the north tower. The 'Hall of Generals' with its embracing twelve columns and arches bears more than a passing resemblance to Wieland Wagner's 1937 *Parsifal* set featuring the Grail temple. It has been suggested that the twelve columns and twelve pedestals were inspired by the belief there were twelve 'Knights of the Round Table'. The crypt has been likened to the set of a 1953 Hollywood movie *Knights of the Round Table* and the Grail Castle as depicted in *Parsifal*.

All this having been said, as Jan Erik Schulte, a historian at the Ruhr University in Bochum and organiser of an exhibition at Wewelsburg, observed 'It's an impressive example of how the SS and its architects tried to falsify and recreate history to justify their own ideology'.[2]

In all, the works cost a total of 13 million reichsmarks. But the bigger price paid was the loss of liberty and life by those who built it. Around 3,900 prisoners, comprising Jews, Jehovah's Witnesses and prisoners of war, were interred in the camp to carry out the work, of whom at least 1,285 died of hunger, disease, cold and maltreatment.

Wewlesburg Castle today.

Reich commander of the SS, Heinrich Himmler, after a visit at Wewelsburg in 1937.

The 'Hall of the SS Generals' in the northern tower of Wewelsburg Castle.

The crypt beneath the hall in the northern tower.

The original set of the Grail Castle from the 1882 Bayreuth production of *Parsifal*.

Camelot on the set of the 1953 film *Knights of the Round Table*.

Chapter 7

Religious Implications of the Grail Hunt

There is some irony in the Nazi Party, a party guilty of treating Jesus's teachings with utter contempt, being hell-bent on capturing perhaps the most sought-after Christian relic. Himmler's actions, as a Nazi, were completely at odds with what we might perceive as a Christian upbringing, but as a 19-year-old, he wrote in his diary 'Come what may, I shall always love God, pray to him and adhere to the Catholic church and defend it, even if I should be expelled from it'. There is a hint here that the young Himmler had a foreboding that someday his personal views would be at odds with those of the church, but he would see the church as having expelled him rather than him having rejected the teachings of the church.

There is no doubt the primary motivation the Nazis had for hunting down the Grail was to emulate the feats of Parsifal. However, there was likely a more pragmatic consideration contemplated as well. In 1933, there were 45 million Protestants and 22 million Catholic Christians in Germany. Finding a Christian artefact as revered as the Holy Grail would bring acclaim to the German nation and a huge sense of pride to its largely Christian population.

It is often claimed that because of the atrocities they committed and the ancient Germanic heritage they asserted the Nazis were pagans. This was not the case, certainly not for the vast majority.

In 1920, the Nazis promoted their version of Christianity, point 24 of the NDSAP (the name by which the Nazis were originally known) Party Program stated:

A doll's house kitchen decorated in wallpaper adorned with images of the Hitler Youth participating a variety of camp activities.

The bedroom with an image of the Madonna and Child hung above thc bed.

In the living room, a picture of the Führer hangs on the wall, garnished with miniature swastika flags.

> *'We demand freedom for all religious confessions in the state, in so far as they do not endanger its existence or conflict with the customs and moral sentiments of the Germanic race. The party as such represents the standpoint of a positive Christianity, without tying itself to a particular confession.'*[1]

Essentially, what the Nazis termed 'positive Christianity' was anti-Semitic. This is made abundantly clear in the next phrase given in the Party Program: 'It fights the spirit of Jewish materialism.'

A corrupted version of Christianity pervaded the Nazi Party throughout its life. Hitler's *Mein Kampf*, written in 1923, was edited by a Catholic priest. The Nazi's leading anti-Semitic propagandist, Julius Streicher, was also the author of works connecting German history with the lives of Christian martyrs. More significantly, when the Allies liberated survivors of the concentration camps, they found hymn books and rosary beads in the quarters of the Nazi officials.

The Deutsches Historisches Museum in Berlin contains an exhibit that reinforces the fact that a warped belief in Christianity, in this instance Roman Catholicism, played a significant role in the home life of at least some avidly Nazi families. A doll's house crafted in 1933 by an anonymous party member contains an abundance of Nazi symbolism. The doll's house is comprised of three rooms, open to the front and adjacent to each other. The kitchen, on the left, is decorated in wallpaper adorned with images of the Hitler Youth participating in a variety of camp activities, including camp cooking, marching and dancing. The kitchen also has on the wall a framed photographic image of Hitler and Mussolini, stood shoulder to shoulder, dressed in full military uniform. In the living room, on the right, a picture of the Führer hangs on the wall, garnished with miniature swastika flags. However, centre stage to the doll's house is the bedroom with an image of the Madonna and Child hanging above the bed.

With regards to the views of the Nazi Party itself, Alfred Rosenburg was a leading Nazi ideologist; he had deputised for Hitler when he was imprisoned after the Beer Hall Putsch and thereafter was a key policy maker regarding racial and religious matters. While imprisoned at Nuremburg before being hung for crimes against humanity, Rosenberg, perhaps seeking some form of clemency, wrote detailed memoirs of his career in the Nazi Party. The following passages add weight to the idea that the Nazis adopted a pragmatic approach regarding Christianity:

> *'At the focal point of all spiritual-psychological discussion stands Christianity, its personages, its relationship to the peoples and to the problems of our epoch. Was my attitude wrong, then, in the face of existing realities, in the face of the dignity inherent in durable historic figures? Or possibly even harmful, perhaps because existing social ties really should be preserved in these days of great fermentation, in contrast to my own persistent opposition to the churches and Christian dogma?*
>
> *'In my works I postulated that I was against all propaganda for leaving the Church, since Christianity is ennobled by the beliefs and the deaths of so many generations. Nobody can expect more tolerance. Basically, the National Socialist movement was obliged to be tolerant; but each single individual could claim for himself the identical freedom of conscience which the churches apparently consider their exclusive property. In 1933, Hitler concluded the concordat with the Vatican. Though personally not a participant, I considered this treaty completely justified.'*[2]

Rosenburg also referenced the influence of Wagner and *Parsifal* on the religious thinking of the Nazis when mentioning his dealings with Hans Schemm, party leader for the Nazis in Bavaria and founder of the National Socialists Teacher's League:

> *'Hans Schemm was a teacher totally under the spell of Bayreuth's music, and particularly, as I found out in 1924, of Parsifal. In 1933, he became Bavarian Secretary of Education, and started out on a consciously Christian course. His old motto. Our politics are Germany,*

our religion is Christ, was honourable; but in its official tone he went far beyond the tolerance agreed upon.'[3]

The Nazis succeeded in manipulating the church in Germany by bargaining and by suppressing dissenters. They set up the Reich church and put at its head a Nazi bishop, Ludwig Muller, to unify the different branches of Protestantism. Hitler made a deal with the Pope that he would leave the Catholic church in Germany alone, and in return, the Pope would stay out of German politics. In 1934, Martin Niemöller, a Protestant cleric who had initially supported the Nazis, set up the Confessing Church in opposition to the Reich church and openly criticised Nazism. Niemöller, along with 800 pastors of the confessional church, was sent to a concentration camp.

A former cellmate at one of the concentration camps where Niemöller was held, Leo Stein, after being released and allowed to go to America, wrote an article about Niemöller for *The National Jewish Monthly* in 1941. Stein reports having asked Niemöller why he ever supported the Nazi Party, to which Niemöller replied:

'I find myself wondering about that too. I wonder about it as much as I regret it. Still, it is true that Hitler betrayed me. I had an audience with him, as a representative of the Protestant Church, shortly before he became Chancellor, in 1932. Hitler promised me on his word of honour, to protect the Church, and not to issue any anti-Church laws. He also agreed not to allow pogroms [mass slaughters] against the Jews, assuring me as follows: "There will be restrictions against the Jews, but there will be no ghettos, no pogroms, in Germany."

'I really believed, given the widespread anti-Semitism in Germany, at that time – that Jews should avoid aspiring to Government positions or seats in the Reichstag. There were many Jews, especially among the Zionists, who took a similar stand. Hitler's assurance satisfied me at the time. On the other hand, I hated the growing atheistic movement, which was fostered and promoted by the Social Democrats and the

> *Communists. Their hostility toward the Church made me pin my hopes on Hitler for a while.*
>
> *'I am paying for that mistake now; and not me alone, but thousands of other persons like me.'*[14]

We should remember these are words attributed to Niemöller while he was still held in a concentration camp, but they do offer an insight into how Hitler manipulated the church in Germany.

What the Nazis attempted to do was to assimilate the Christian church into their doctrine and in doing so create the myth of Aryan divinity.

Chapter 8

Rahn's Theory and the Cathars

Rahn set out his theory, defining the whereabouts of the Grail, in his book *Crusade Against the Grail.* Whilst Rahn was a passionate, intelligent and thorough researcher with an eye for detail, the aforementioned culmination of his work is less a coherent, reasoned argument and more a composition of poetic ramblings interspersed with observations and conclusions. In any case, Rahn's theory hinged on the belief that the source for Wolfram von Eschenbach's *Parzival* or *Parsifal* was a medieval troubadour named Kyot, hailing from the Provence region of France:

> *'Now Kyot laschantiure was the name*
> *Of one whose art compelled him*
> *To tell what shall gladden no few.*
> *Kyot is that noted Provencal*
> *Who saw this Tale of Parsifal*
> *Written in that heathenish tongue.*
> *And what he retold in French*
> *I shall not be too dull*
> *To recount in German'.*[1]

Rahn identifies Kyot as a troubadour from northern France, Guyot de Provins, who Rahn reckons at one time plied his trade in Carcassonne, the medieval fortified city near Provence.

Rahn claims that Kyot was known to Wolfram but not known to Chrétien de Troyes, the author of *Perceval le Gallois* (the French version of the tale). Therefore, Wolfram's version of the tale was more definitive.

Comparing texts, Rahn deduces that Herzeloyde (Parzival's mother) was the Viscountess Adelaide de Carcassonne, a widowed mother with a son named Raimon Roger.

Furthermore, Rahn equates Trencavel with the widow Adelaide's son, Raimon Roger. The Raimon Roger in question was, in fact, a member of the noble Trencaval family and, therefore, can be referred to as Raimon Roger Trencaval to distinguish him from other Raimon Rogers of noble birth, of which there was at least another one coinciding with this time. Rahn chose to focus on the Trencavel connection, with his claim that Wolfram translated this as 'pierce through the heart', whilst also claiming this was the meaning of the titular name Parsifal, and thus claims that Raimon Roger was Wolfram's model for his Parzival.

In summary:

Viscountess Adelaide de Carcassonne = Herzeloyde
Viscountess Adelaide de Carcassonne's son = Trencavel
Trencavel = Parzival
Raimon Roger = Trencavel
Therefore, Raimon Roger = Parzival

Rahn believed the young Raimon was educated by his mother, Adelaide, and a Cathar heretic, Bertran de Saissac, at the request of his father, Roger Taillefer. This is true in that Bertran de Saissac acted as young Raimon's guardian after the death of his father in 1194. Rahn asserts that young Raimon was bound for a higher purpose from an early age:

'A son who was destined never to become an ordinary knight, but a knight of the supreme Minne [courtly love]. He had to be worthy of the "Round Table" in Montségur, that inaccessible Pyrenean castle of carved rock where the Pure Doctrine of the Consoling Paraclete was preserved:

Upon my word you are Parsifal!
Your name means. "Pierce-in-the-heart"
Great love ploughed just such a furrow

Through your mother's heart …
Your father left sorrow for her portion
Wolfram von Eschenbach

Parsifal had to show himself worthy of the Knights of the Grail!'[2]

The 'Pure Doctrine of the Consoling Paraclete' to which Rahn refers is Catharism or Albigensianism (Albigensianism being derived from the Cathars association with the city of Albi); the faith which swept across the Languedoc, a region of southern France in the Middle Ages.

The main premise behind the Cathar faith was the rejection of materialism. This belief was taken to such an extent that they believed all things material were evil, created by an evil God sometimes referred to as 'Rex Mundi' or 'King of the World'. They were dualists in that they also believed there was a good God, a God of Light and Spirit. Rahn was aware of the dualist beliefs held by the Cathars and often referred to this in terms of Lucifer being the devil incarnate. This is a common theme throughout his writing. Time and again, he uses references to Lucifer as a nod to the dualism of the Cathar faith to which he felt a close affinity. One such example is given by Rahn when he describes Raimon's mother, Adelaide, in *Crusade Against the Grail.* He says: 'For her, (Adelaide) the threatening God of Israel was Lucifer. Adelaide was a Heretic!'[3]

The Cathars believed that people were imperfect spirits captured in an evil body. They believed in reincarnation and that heaven could only be reached by living a perfect life, devoid of material trappings. The strictest adherents to the faith were known as perfects, who committed to a life of self-denial, whereas most believers were freer to do pretty much as they pleased within the context of living a good life as set out in the gospels of the New Testament. Men and women were equals and authority was shunned. Aside from the perfects, who were akin to living saints, the Cathar faith consisted of a rather loose confederation of ordinary people, with differing backgrounds, sympathetic to the religion, rather than a uniformity of devout followers of the creed. To many, Catharism must have been a release from the strict jurisdiction of the Catholic church. Nobles must surely have seen being set free from paying tithes to the church as an incentive to join the Cathar faith. Whatever the circumstances, the faith really took hold in the Languedoc region of France, as well as in areas of Spain, Italy and Germany, in the late-twelfth and early-thirteenth centuries. This constituted a major threat to the established Catholic church. Unsurprisingly, the Catholic church viewed the Cathars or Albigensians as heretics, and in 1209, Pope Innocent III announced a crusade against them. A crusade that came to be known as the Albigensian Crusade. 'Kill them all, God will know his own!' these were the words attributed to Arnold Amaury, the monk leading the crusade, as the crusaders set forth.

Raimon Roger Trencavel (1188–1209) was a key figure in the Cathar story, who was sympathetic to the Cathars. In 1209, he stood alone in defending the Cathars against the northern nobles. When the Albigensian Crusade began in 1209, Raimon Roger Trencavel was 24 years old and the Viscount of Albi, Carcassonne, Béziers and Razes. Raimon Roger mounted his stand against the crusade at Carcassonne in the heart of his territories.

Before the crusaders reached Carcassonne, they sacked Béziers and showed no mercy to the residents of the city, slaughtering 20,000 of them in cold blood. Upon hearing this, Raimon Roger immediately implemented a scorched-earth policy in a bid to make the lands surrounding Carcassonne as inhospitable for the crusaders as they could be. For miles around the city, he ordered every windmill be destroyed, every crop burned and every animal slaughtered.

When the crusaders arrived and camped in tents outside the city walls, beyond the range of the defender's crossbows, they massively outnumbered the combatants inside the citadel. Before long, having secured an entrance to the city by defeating the defenders of Bourg, a settlement below the city walls, the Crusaders were poised to mount an onslaught on Carcassonne.

However, at the eleventh hour, 100 armoured horsemen arrived, nobles of Catalonia and Aragon. Their leader, King Pedro, had impeccable Catholic credentials and was welcomed by the crusaders into their camp. But Raimon Roger was a distant feudal relative of King Pedro, and it was Raimon Roger that he had come to see. King Pedro was highly regarded by the Pope, and the crusaders were in no real position to argue with him.

Unarmed, and with only three fellow riders, Pedro approached the city walls, as he did so the drawbridge was lowered. Raimon Roger welcomed Pedro into the city with open arms. The two had met in the city five years earlier when Pedro had tried to dissuade Raimon Roger from tolerating Cathars. The two parleyed once again, and when Pedro returned to the besiegers camped outside the city sought to persuade the leader of the crusaders, Arnold Amaury, to relinquish his siege. Amaury said that he would allow Raimon Roger and eleven companions of his choosing to leave the city with whatever they could carry and that the fate of the remaining inhabitants of the city would then be left to the discretion of the crusaders. Pedro was aghast at the miserly offer made by Amaury and replied with short shrift 'donkeys will fly' before Raimon agreed to such a deal.

When Pedro put the deal to Raimon the next day, it was rebuffed at once, with Raimon declaring he would rather be flayed alive than betray his people by leaving their fate to the crusaders who had administered genocide to the inhabitants of neighbouring Béziers. With this, the crusaders began their attack and stormed the suburb of Castellar laying between them and the main city of Carcassonne. But the attack was unsuccessful, and the crusaders were driven back. They then resorted to breaching the walls of the suburb by tunnelling. A vicious fight ensued in which most of Castellar's defenders were killed. The suburb was secured by the crusaders with a skeleton guard, and most of the northern lords forming their number returned to their encampment, pleased with their day's work.

Raimon Roger and his men seized the opportunity to counterattack and won back Castellar. But, before Raimon's men had massacred all the crusaders left to guard Castellar in revenge for the genocide they had committed at Béziers, hundreds of mounted knights came riding out of the crusader camp. The Carcassonnais could not withstand them and retreated inside the city walls, shutting the gate smartly behind them.

The siege now began in earnest. When the Carcassonnais had lost control of the settlement of Bourg the previous week, they lost with it their supply of fresh water. The August weather was unforgiving, and the city soon became bone dry, with what little water there was quickly became wretched and stagnant. Sickness and death spread throughout the city; suffering was everywhere. With the siege taking its toll, a lone rider rode out from the crusader encampment and approached the walls of the city. He proclaimed to those guarding the walls that he was a kinsman of Raimon Roger. This was acknowledged by the guards and the rider was let in.

Viscount Raymond Roger Trencavel arrested in treason by order of the legate, engraving (1862), private collection.

Raymond Roger Trencavel.

The noble expressed his understanding to Raimon, of the defender's predicament, but then warned him of the possible consequences of holding out and reminded Raimon what had happened to the inhabitants of Béziers. Raimon agreed that suing for peace was the best course of action and rode alone out of the city into the crusader's camp. He was ushered into the tent of a leading crusader, Herve de Donzy. He would never be a free man again. The people of Carcassonne were set free and allowed to leave the city, but as one chronicler put it, 'Not even the value of a button were they allowed to take with them.'[4]

With the city cleared, Raimon was brought back into Carcassonne in chains. He was imprisoned in his own dungeon and was dead within three months. The cause of death provided by his captors was dysentery, but rumours of foul play abounded. Raimon had long been a Cathar sympathiser and a thorn in the side of the church. As far as the church were concerned, he was better out of the way for good. Rahn, for his part, asserts that Raimon was poisoned and with his death and the fall of Carcassonne – the Grail was in danger!

The Albigensian Crusade went on for another twenty years, stamping out the Cathar faith across the Languedoc, the region in the south of France that was home to Raimon Roger, in cities such as Toulouse, Narbonne and Montpellier. This was followed by fifteen years of oppression and resistance, culminating in the last stand of the Cathars at the mountain fortress of Montségur.

Avignonet – 'Where is my cup?'

In the aftermath of the Albigensian Crusade, the church was relentless in sending out inquisitors to Languedoc to root out any flickering cinders that might kindle the wildfire of Catharism. This perpetuated a feeling of fear and resentment among the Occitans, a name referring to the language they spoke and given to the natives of Languedoc.

It was only a matter of time before things would come to a head, and they did on 28 May 1242. Two inquisitors, Stephen of St Thibery and William Arnald, were being billeted in the keep of the castle at Avignonet, a town between Toulouse and Carcassonne. Their host at the castle, the town bailiff, Raymond D'Alfaro, was to be complicit in their murder. As night fell, D'Alfaro sent one of his men, William-Raymond Golairan, to check on his visitors. Seeing that the inquisitors were settled in the chamber assigned to them, enjoying their evening meal, Golairan, slipped away from the castle and into the nearby woods.

There, as had been pre-arranged, he met a posse of heavily armed men from Montségur led by Peter Roger. Roger selected a few dozen of his men to ride back to Avignonet with Golairan, while he and the remainder of his party stayed and watched out for any incoming French knights.

When they reached Avignonet, the raiders dismounted and tethered their horses before hiding behind a slaughterhouse on the outskirts of the town outside the walls. Golairan returned to the castle keep and checked on the inquisitors once again. Seeing they were fast asleep, he made his way back to the ramparts and opened the gate for the armed men to come in.

The men of Montségur slipped into the town, under the cover of darkness, and made their way through the cobbled streets to the castle keep, where around thirty local townsmen joined them. With the Cathar credentes or believers William de Lahille, William de Baguier and Bernard de St Martin leading the way, the united band of henchmen continued through the corridors and stairways of the keep to the chamber where the inquisitors lay sleeping. The assailants burst into the room and swayed their axes, knives or clubs into the bodies sleeping there. Then rifling through a chest, the inquisitors had brought with them, they found an inquisition register. Promptly, they ripped the register up and set it alight before leaving the keep. The men from Montségur rushed back to where their horses were tethered and made good their escape.

When they reached the woods where Peter Roger was waiting, they were greeted with unbridled enthusiasm. Roger exclaimed 'Where is my cup?' One of the raiding party replied 'It is broken.' Unable to contain his laughter, Roger retorted 'Traitor! I would have bound it together with a circlet of gold and drunk from it all my days!'

The cup the men discussed was the skull of William Arnald, one of the two inquisitors the raiders had just hacked to death. Years earlier, Arnald had burned alive 210 Cathars he had found in hiding at a village named Moissac.

Montségur

The war party were welcomed back to Montségur with much joy. The inquisitors were both hated and feared, the deaths of Stephen of St Thibery and William Arnald were something to be celebrated. News of the killings spread quickly; a spark had been lit and soon a spirit of revolt engulfed the Languedoc.

Count Raymond VII of Toulouse, a Cathar sympathiser, was now seen by many as being the man in charge of the region, having been marginalized by the church following Catharism being effectively stamped out by the Albigensian Crusade. But the people of Toulouse were betrayed by Roger Bernard of Foix, who had distinguished himself in the fight against the Albigensian Crusade. Feeling that the revolt was madness, a doomed venture that would bring untold recriminations and suffering to his people, Roger Bernard made his own peace with the French in the autumn of 1242. This left Raymond of Toulouse out on a limb and, seeing that there was no point in leading his people into a conflict they had no chance of winning, signed a treaty with Louis VII of France that amounted to little more than a slap on the wrist.

The French nobility may have been fine with this, but the church was not. They were still smarting from the murder of the two inquisitors and were intent on revenge. The eyes of the church were firmly set on Montségur. This was the only place in the Languedoc that still openly practised Catharism. Montségur was the place the church referred to as the 'Synagogue of Satan'. In a conclave held in 1243, the church decided that it was Montségur that had to pay.

Inside the mountaintop fortress at Montségur were some 200 perfects, but they were not alone. Living among the perfects were men-at-arms and their families. Many of the men-at-arms had relatives among the perfects, others had been made homeless by the tyranny of the Albigensian Crusade and some were mercenaries. The leader of these men-at arms and lord of Montségur was Peter Roger of Mirepoix, who had led the raiding party responsible for the murders of the inquisitors at Avignonet.

A myriad of troops began to gather in the pastures to the east of Montségur at the behest of Henri of Arcis, the agent of the crown at Carcassonne, acting on behalf of the church. There were soldiers from Gascony and Aquitaine as well as men freshly press ganged into service from Languedoc. Yet for all these men being at their disposal, the besiegers were still unable to completely encircle Montségur. The base of the mountain had a craggy perimeter of over two miles in length over rough terrain that was impossible to seal completely. This afforded the defenders of Montségur some opportunity for communication with the world outside.

With the perfects unable to fight, Peter Roger had a mere ninety-eight soldiers at his disposal to defend the fortress, but the steep terrain surrounding the citadel was in his favour; there was no possibility of the attackers using siege engines and all other methods by which they might mount an assault were perilous. Any assaults the attackers did mount were seen off with arrows and other projectiles raining down on them from the walls of the castle. And so, spring, summer and autumn passed, with the defenders having lost twelve of their number but their walls unbreeched.

As winter closed in on the besiegers, Henri of Arcis decided it was time to take a risk. A commando-style operation was mounted, at night under the cover of darkness while many of the defenders lay sleeping, with a group of men from Gascon scaling the steep cliffs that led to a bastion atop Roc de la Tour, a few hundred yards to the east of the main fortress at Montségur. This was no easy climb; the troops were weighed down and encumbered with heavy arms and the route was treacherous throughout. They could all have easily been lost for no gain, but the men from Gascon made it and took the defenders inside the bastion by surprise. The defenders were quickly dispatched, and the bastion was taken.

It was now only a matter of time before Montségur fell. Bertrand Marty, the spiritual leader of the perfects inside Montségur, hastily arranged for the treasure belonging to the sect to be smuggled out before it was taken. Four perfects were charged with the responsibility of getting the treasure to safety and this they did under the cover of night, slipping through the net of the besiegers.

With Roc de la Tour secured, the attackers hoisted up armaments and bombarded the defenders of Montségur. The incessant barrage took its toll, and with the defender's heads kept down, the attacker's entrenchments inched ever closer to the walls of the crumbling citadel.

In February 1244, the last messenger to reach Montségur from the outlying lowlands arrived. He urged the defenders to hold out, for help in the form of an army led by Count Raymond of Toulouse might yet arrive in time to save them. Alas, the defenders short of food and ammunition, exhausted by their travails, were not able to hold out any longer.

On 2 March 1244, the fortress gate opened, and Peter Roger walked out waving the white flag of surrender. The armistice saw a two-week truce declared after which the lay people, including those who had participated in the murders at Avignonet, would be free to go subject to them co-operating with the inquisition. But for the perfects no mercy was to be shown, unless they recanted their beliefs, something they were never going to do. The perfects would be burned to death.

Such was the strength of belief in their cause that before the end of the two-week truce, twenty-one of the lay people or credentes approached Bertrand Marty and asked to be made perfects. Among their number were three ladies of nobility, including Corba and her daughter Esclarmonde, one peasant woman, four knights, six other men-at-arms and two of their wives, two messengers, one squire, one crossbowman and one merchant. All were welcomed into the ranks of the perfects, and on 16 March 1244, a line of around 220 perfects wound their way down the track from Montségur to the lowlands beneath, where a gruesome death awaited them.

In his book, *Crusade Against the Grail*, Rahn recounts the siege at Montségur and the events leading up to it, before focussing on the 'treasure' smuggled out before the fortress was taken.

> *'The night of the fall of Montségur, a fire was seen on the snowy summit of Bidorta. It was not an execution pyre, but a fire of happiness. Four Cathars, of whom three are known to us – Amiel Aicart, Poitevin, and Hugo – were signalling the Perfecti of Montségur, who were about to die, that the Muni was safe.*
>
> *From the documents of the Inquisitors of Carcassonne, it is surmised that these four Pure Ones, covered in wool blankets, descended on ropes from the summit of the promontory to the bottom of the Lasset gorge to hand the treasure of the heretics to a Son of Belissena, Pons-Arnaud de Castellum Verdunum, in the Sabarthes.*
>
> *The "treasure of the heretics"?*
>
> *Since Peire Roger de Mirepoix was given permission to take all the gold and silver with him, what the four intrepid Cathars brought to safety in the caves of the Sabarthes, an area that belonged to the lords of Castellum Verdunum, was certainly not gold or silver.*
>
> *Amiel Aicart, Poitevin, Hugo and the fourth knight, whose name is unknown, were the grandchildren of those wise Celt Iberians who in other times threw the treasure of Delphi to the bottom of lake Tabor. As Cathars they would have preferred to take the pathway to the stars together with their brothers in the fire of the camp des cramats. As they climbed the pathway of the Cathars that crosses the "valley of*

enchantment" bordering the lake of the druids and ascends abruptly toward the Tabor and Bidorta they must have seen the blazing flames of Montségur to the north. What they were safeguarding was neither gold nor silver; it was the "Desire for Paradise"...

This is how the Grail, the Occitan Mani, was brought to safety in the caves of Ornolac.[5]

Chapter 9

Christian Relic?

The Occitan Mani to which Rahn refers is what he earlier describes as a symbol borrowed by the Cathars from the Buddhists of Nepal. The symbol is a precious stone, representative of God, which illuminates the world with its flashing. In making this hypothesis, Rahn draws another key conclusion: 'It is clear that the Grail of Chrétien de Troyes, Guyot and Wolfram has nothing to do with the Last Supper or a 'Christian' relic … The Grail was a heretical symbol.'[1]

In referring to the Grail as a heretical symbol, Rahn was beginning to get closer to the truth. When stories of the Grail were revived in the nineteenth century, both in Arthurian romances and in the operatic works of Wagner, including *Parsifal*, the Grail was identified as the Holy Grail, or cup of Christ, consistent with the model of the grail provided in Sir Thomas Malory's *Le Morte D'Arthur*, which was the culmination of the medieval Grail romances.

The revival of interest in Arthurian romances in the nineteenth century was sparked in 1816 when Malory's work was reprinted for the first time since the sixteenth century. This inspired poets, the most pre-eminent of whom was Alfred Lord Tennyson, to develop the themes set out in Malory's work. Tennyson's Arthurian works were published in *Idylls of the King*, a cycle of twelve narrative poems, between 1859 and 1885. Below is an excerpt from the eighth of these poems 'The Holy Grail: The Tragedy of Percivale':

'To whom the monk: "The Holy Grail – I trust
We are green in Heaven's eyes; but here too much
We moulder – as to things without I mean –
Yet one of your own knights, a guest of ours,
Told us of this in our refectory,
But spake with such a sadness and so low
We heard not half of what he said. What is it?
The phantom of a cup that comes and goes?"

"Nay, monk! What phantom?" answered Percivale.
"The cup, the cup itself, from which our Lord
Drank at the last sad supper with his own."'[2]

It is abundantly clear here that the Grail portrayed by Tennyson is the cup used by Christ at the Last Supper. The monk engaged in conversation with Percivale is earlier named as Ambrosius by Tennyson. This an interesting take on the role played by Ambrosius Aurelianus, who led the British in their struggles against the Saxons in the fifth century, in the legend of King Arthur. In his work, *The History of the Kings of Britain*, a pseudohistory written in 1136, Geoffrey of Monmouth casts him as the paternal uncle of King Arthur.

Similarly, in Prelude to Act I of *Parsifal*, Wagner strongly alludes to the Grail being the cup associated with the Last Supper:

'Take ye my body, take my blood, in token of our love!' (Repeated in faint whispers by angel-voices.)

'Take ye my blood, my body take, in memory of me!' (Again, repeated in whispers.)[3]

Wagner's widow, Cosima referenced the significance of the Grail in his work in an entry written in her diary on 26 September 1877:

> *'He plays me the Prelude, from the orchestral sketch! My emotion lasts long – then he speaks to me about this feature, in the mystery of the Grail, of blood turning into wine, which permits us to turn our gaze refreshed back to earth, whereas the conversion of wine into blood draws us away from the earth.'*[4]

However, the Grail only became a Christian relic in around 1190, when the unfinished work of Chrétien de Troyes was continued by other authors, and it then became the cup of the Last Supper.

Despite what Rahn says in concluding his prologue about the word Grail 'being obscure from the beginning', it is made clear by him referring earlier to the object of his search as the 'Holy Grail' that in the first instance the object he set out to find was the cup of the Last Supper.

The wider belief in the Nazi Party that the Grail Parsifal sought was indeed the 'Holy Grail' is evidenced by the gleaming cross depicted in the background of the 1933 stamp issued in Nazi Germany, with Parsifal bearing the Grail centre stage.

A German postage stamp issued in 1933, bearing the likeness of Parsifal holding the Holy Grail.

Chapter 10

Rahn's Search for the Grail Continues

Rahn was now on the payroll of the SS, and his expeditions, searching out further clues as to the whereabouts of the Grail, were funded unquestionably by the Reich, a measure of both their faith in Rahn and their desire to get their hands on the Grail. In

Rahn's handler, 'Weisthor' Karl Maria Wiligut.

a somewhat clandestine set-up, Rahn's reports were funnelled back to Hitler through a third-party, Karl Maria Wiligut, a brigadier in the SS on Himmler's personal staff, who among other things happened to believe that Christ was a German. Wiligut, who was also known by the alias Weisthor, or 'wizard', was a key man in the cultural development of the SS, with some rather strange beliefs. Wiligut believed that Jesus was in fact Baldur, the ancient Germanic god, and that when Baldur was crucified by worshipers of the rival god Wotan, he escaped death and fled to the Middle East, where his story is taken up in the New Testament. It was Wiligut who designed the death's head ring or *Totenkopfring* that adorned SS uniforms. He had also been central to the development of Wewelsburg as the headquarters of the SS. In the years that followed, Rahn developed a close relationship with his handler. A relationship that would eventually end fatally for both.

During his time in the Languedoc, Rahn had been drawn into the doctrine of the Cathars, they had become heroes to him, and this clouded his thinking. Obsessed by the link he perceived between the Cathars and the legend of Parzival, Rahn initially limited his investigations to France, before expanding them into Spain and Italy. In these countries, he was essentially searching places to which he thought the Cathars could have smuggled the Grail. In a somewhat ad hoc manner, he picked up on local legends taking him from one town or city to another.

We can gain knowledge of where Rahn's continuation of his search for the Grail took him from a work he published titled *The Court of Lucifer*. The title of which stems from Rahn's growing belief that the Grail was not the cup used by Christ at the Last Supper to share his blood but a stone that had become dislodged from the crown of Lucifer. This is another nod to the dualist beliefs of the Cathar faith.

> *'As far as the Grail is concerned, it must be, as many believe, a stone fallen from Lucifer's crown. This is why the Church vindicated it in their turn, to Christianise this Luciferian symbol. Montségur's pog was*

> *the mountain of the Grail, of which Esclarmonde was mistress. After her death, after the destruction of Montségur and the extermination of the Cathars, the Grail and its castle were abandoned. The Church, perfectly aware with the Albigensian Crusade of leading, first of all, a war of the Cross against the Grail, let no opportunity slip of appropriating this new non-Christian religious symbol for itself and milking it for all it was worth. But this was not enough to explain that the Grail was the chalice that Jesus had shared with his disciples at the Last Supper and in which his blood had been.'*[1]

Esclarmonde was a noble lady who had been made a perfect, one of the Cathar creed's most priestly class, in the dying days of the siege at Montségur. Rahn saw her as a kind Grail Queen.

Rahn had long believed that a link had existed between the Cathars dualist beliefs and Lucifer, the fallen angel whose vanity had led to him loving himself more than he loved God. In *Crusade Against the Grail*, Rahn refers to a passage from *Parzival*:

> '*When Lucifer made the descent to hell*
> *With his following, a man succeeded him.*'[2]

Rahn believed that man came about when God granted reprieve to the angels who had followed Lucifer to earth. Rahn then drew the tenuous conclusion that the Grail, or Occitan Mani, was a jewel that had fallen from the crown of Lucifer.

In *Lucifer Court*, Rahn explains that after a brief sojourn in Paris, he returned to the Languedoc, to its capital at Toulouse. There, Rahn visited the square where it was said a stone had slain Simon de Montfort. De Montfort was a knight who been part of the Albigensian Crusade from the very start and had distinguished himself to such an extent at the siege of Carcassonne that when Raimon Roger Trencavel, Rahn's Parzival, died a prisoner in his own dungeon, he was given his lands by Arnold Amaury, the leader of the crusaders. Rahn asserts that he was told 'a heroic Toulousan' with a steady hand manoeuvred a stone from the ramparts and felled the hated de Montfort.

Travelling on to Pamiers, Rahn heard tales of a rival seeker of the Grail. An engineer from Bordeaux, who at that very moment was mounting his own search for the Grail in Montségur. Rahn made plans to return to Montségur but on his way there stopped off at Lavelanet, where he encountered an octogenarian local, Mr Rives. Rahn was enticed back to the house of his new acquaintance by tales of a collection of artefacts the old resident of Lavelanet had discovered in a lifetime of trawling the hills and grottoes surrounding Montségur. When he examined the hoard, he found it mainly consisted of weapons and projectiles hurled down in defence of the fortress by the Cathars, along with some mysterious clay doves, which Rahn, not surprised, found himself relating to a passage from Eschenbach's great work. But then the host revealed to Rahn that a deceased friend had once discovered an ancient book at the castle with characters that were unrecognisable to him. Unfortunately, the ancient book had subsequently been lost, but intrigued by the prospect of perhaps finding what messages might have been contained it, Rahn hastened his journey to Montségur.

When he arrived in Montségur, Rahn caught up with his rival, the engineer from Bordeaux. Although guarded in what he said, the engineer told Rahn that a diviner, acting on his behalf, had located the whereabouts of a tomb, where the engineer believed treasure lay hidden. Rahn was put at ease by what the engineer told him, believing that the engineer would never find the Grail because it was hidden in a grotto, not a sarcophagus. His confidence was reaffirmed by a conversation he had with a local shepherd who assured him that the Grail had at one time been kept inside the walls of the castle at Montségur when it was still standing and then poured scorn on the claims of the diviner, who the engineer from Bordeaux was pinning his hopes on.

Rahn though, was prevented from continuing his search for the Grail due to heavy snow. Undaunted, he used the break to take inspiration from Parzival, musing in *The Court of Lucifer*: 'The object of Parzival's nostalgic quest is the Grail, a stone of light, which would make any terrestrial light seem dull, and which would correspond to the realisation of all terrestrial desires, Paradise. The one who sees the Grail cannot die.'

After several attempts to resume his search for the Grail in the caves around Montségur were thwarted by snow, Rahn retired to Lavelanet, where he caught up with Mr Rives. A discussion they had led Rahn to the convoluted belief that King Arthur's Round Table was a euphemism for the perfect 'circle' of the Cathars, and furthermore, Arthur's 'circle' was the Grail. Rahn patently identified Eschenbach's Parzival with Sir Percival, the knight of King Arthur's Round Table. Both the tales of King Arthur and the Knights of the Round Table and Eschenbach's tale of Parzival were familiar to Rahn from infancy, embedded in his memory by his mother reading them to him as a child. When Mr Rives told Rahn of his firm belief that Montségur was the 'Grail Castle', Rahn was clearly buoyed and his enthusiasm for the search rejuvenated.

With renewed ardour, Rahn proceeded to Carcassonne, where he investigated the siege that was the last stand of Raimon Roger Trencavel, the Cathar figure Rahn believed was the historical Parzival. Rahn asserted that Trencavel was betrayed by the crusaders when he was tricked into entering their camp to engage in negotiations under the promise of safe passage, only to be seized and imprisoned. He then concluded that Trencavel met his end when he was poisoned by Simon de Montfort the crusader who most benefitted from his capture, having been given his lands and castle, following the siege. Rahn at this point, was in many ways gathering facts and forming opinions without necessarily joining the dots.

Rahn's travels then took him to Lombrives, where his muddled thinking led him to countenance the possibility that the caves there were once the site where Eschenbach's Parzival, who Rahn presumably still believes was one and the same as Raimon Roger Trencavel, received a Cathar consecration before he found the salvation of the Grail.

Rahn's search was never far from the legend of Parzival, but with a lack of hard evidence and crucially no sighting of the grail, Rahn's ruminations became evermore wild and his theories evermore outlandish:

> *'Did Heracles find the Grail, the stone of Light? Was he a Hellenic Parzival? I believe so. – For Wolfram von Eschenbach, "Heracles possessed the understanding of stones". In this way, Heracles knew also of the stone fallen from Lucifer's crown, which was called the Grail. In a poem in Old French, a Grail-questing knight's ultimate goal was Olympia. I assert that Heracles entered into the Grail's circle, and Parzival sat at the Olympian gods' table, where they offered him their nectar and ambrosia.'*[3]

It is possible there is some duality of meaning in Rahn's reference to the 'stone fallen from Lucifer's crown'. The obvious interpretation is that the remark references the dualistic beliefs of the Cathars, and this is the inference Rahn most intended to make. However, it is possible that he was also either consciously or subconsciously referring to his own demise having fallen into the Nazi Party, with all its evils, having been brought up in a Christian family.

Throughout his time searching for the Grail of behalf of the Nazis, Rahn dutifully kept in touch with his handler, Weisthor, informing him of his progress. It seems though that Rahn may have been guilty of embellishing his reports with whimsical allusions. In a letter of 27 September 1935 to the Weisthor, marked strictly confidential, Rahn says that he has 'discovered very big surprises'. Whilst he might have uncovered some interesting side notes and developed some fanciful theories, he was yet to unearth anything substantial in terms of concrete evidence as to the specific whereabouts of the Grail. This lack of concrete findings led to Rahn widening his search and considering other options.

Whilst in Marseille, Rahn also briefly countenanced the possibility of the Grail having travelled to Great Britain in the custody of Joseph of Arimathea. There are several legends suggesting that Joseph visited mainland Britain, firstly as a merchant trading for metal, some saying he brought with him the child Jesus, and secondly bringing with him the Holy Grail. We will investigate these legends further in Part II, but it is not long before Rahn drops this line of enquiry, and his thoughts return to Parzival. When he returned to Germany, he visited Berlin and paid a visit to the opera house to take in Wagner's *Parsifal* and *Lohengrin*. On seeing the Grail knight's costume adorned with a turtle emblem, he is reminded of the clay doves belonging to Mr Rives.

Rahn clung desperately to the hope that the legend of Parzival would lead him to finding the Grail, but Montségur had yet to reveal her secret, so he turned to another ancient work of literature, The Eddas, a brace of Icelandic manuscripts, in a bid to find further clues and finally unravel the mystery of the Grail.

The Eddas are two books, *The Prose Edda* (younger) and *The Poetic Edda* (older), both written in the thirteenth century. *The Prose Edda*, written by Snorri, an Icelandic chief judge, poet and historian, is a guide to ancient Icelandic *skalds*, or poems, thought to have originated in Norway around the ninth century. *The Poetic Edda* is a collection of lays (a medieval poem) featuring Germanic heroes, written between AD 800 and 1000. It is believed there may have been some Celtic influence in the writing of these lays. Their authorship is open to debate, with Norsemen, Englishmen and Irishmen all having been suggested as composers.

The Eddas were of great interest to the Weisthor, Karl Maria Wiligut, and he may well have pointed Rahn in their direction. Whatever, Rahn determined to sail to Iceland and establish whatever links he could between the Eddas and the Grail.

The British Edda reconstructed by L.A. Waddell in 1930, was a translation of *The Poetic Edda*, which Waddell believed to be British in origin. The subtitle of this work reads: 'The Great Epic Poem of the Ancient Britons on the Exploits of King Thor, Artur or Adam and his Knights in Establishing Civilization Reforming Eden and Capturing the Holy Grail.'

Whether Rahn was aware of this work or not we do not know. If he was aware of Waddell's words, this must have bolstered his confidence and boosted his belief that he was drawing ever closer to the ultimate prize. What we do know though is that when he sailed across the North Sea bound for Iceland. He first docked in Scotland, where he took time to explore Edinburgh and Arthur's Seat. After scrutinising Arthur's Seat, Rahn felt the impulse to write:

> *'King Arthur, that is Artus, the great king of the North. His chariot is always ready to ferry his own to Lucifer's kingdom, where the luminous asphodel fields are also to be found. The Germans of the North called it "Thorr in a chariot" and the guardian of the force of the gods. Or also the Great Father…'*[14]

Rahn had flitted for a while between trying to claim Christianity as an ancient German religion and dabbling in the occult with pagan references. Weisthor did much the same. Here we find an example of this, with Rahn incorporating Thor and the Great Father in the same passage. Thor is the pagan Norse god; the reference to the Great Father is one to a monotheistic God, contrasting with the gods, and it a Christian vision of God, as in 'Our Father who art in heaven'.

Rahn was within touching distance of finding the truth behind the Grail without realising how close he was. Unaware of just how close he was to finding the truth, Rahn left the shores of Britain and set sail for Iceland. There he visited Reykjavik, Laugarvatn and Reykholt without unearthing any trace of the Grail.

Rahn returned to Germany to complete the journal documenting his travels *The Court of Lucifer: A Voyage with Europe's Benevolent Ghosts* published in 1937. Throughout this work, there is a sense that his voyage had become as much a sightseeing tour, taking in cultural features of the places he visited, as it was a genuine search for the Grail.

Alas, this proved to be yet another unfruitful mission. Rahn returned empty handed to Germany, to complete the journal documenting his travels, a somewhat cryptic account of his adventures entitled *The Court of Lucifer, A Voyage with Europe's Benevolent Ghosts* published in 1937.

In the closing passages of *The Court of Lucifer*, Rahn writes: 'Along with the pages of my Journal on my left, I will also put away the stone which acts as their paperweight. I brought it back, a long time ago now, from the ruins of the Pyrenean heretic fortress of Montségur, the Grail castle.'[5]

There is a marked disparity with the phraseology he had used in closing passages of his earlier work *Crusade Against the Grail* published in 1933: 'What happened to the Grail, the Occitan Mani? ... The present work could not and did not pretend to be an exhaustive study of the subject. ...I am hoping to bring out a second work soon, a continuation of the present one.'[6]

Rahn at his writing desk.

The first passage strongly suggests his search has come to an end, whereas the earlier work gives the impression that he is on to something, and this is just the start of greater things to come. Sadly, for Rahn, it didn't work out this way.

Chapter 11

The Holy Lance

In contrast to Rahn's failed search for the Grail taking place over seven years, Hitler managed to secure the other holy relic central to the plot of *Parsifal*, the Holy Lance, in one fell swoop.

When the Anschluss took place and Austria was annexed by Nazi Germany, Hitler was welcomed into Vienna by most Austrians with open arms. Austria was in recession and the right-wing government seemed incapable of bringing about a recovery. Hitler was seen by the Austrians as a strong leader with a clear economic vision that was proving successful.

The Austrians had yet to see the darker side of the Nazi regime, but it wouldn't be long before they were shown this, with the Nazis wasting no time in persecuting Jews in Austria. As it was, when Hitler entered Vienna on 13 March 1938, he was greeted with rapturous cheering and chants of '*sieg heil*' (victory hail). On arriving in Vienna, Hitler wasted no time in making his way to the Hofmuseum, where, as the new leader, he claimed the Holy Lance or Hofburg Spear. Hitler later described this experience to a group of newspaper reporters:

> *'I knew with immediacy that this was an important moment in my life… I stood there quietly gazing upon it for several minutes quite oblivious to the scene around me. It seemed to carry some hidden inner meaning which evaded me, a meaning which I felt I inwardly knew yet could not bring to consciousness. I felt as though I myself had held it in my hands before in some earlier century in history … that I myself had once claimed it as my talisman of power and held the destiny of the world in my hands.'*[1]

The Anschluss in Vienna. Hitler salutes the welcoming crowd in 1938. In front of him in an SS uniform is Heinrich Himmler.

If this was not Hitler casting himself in the role of Parsifal, then what was it? This was certainly the image portrayed in contemporary Nazi propaganda (see images overleaf).

The dove symbolising the 'holy spirit' in *Parsifal Revealing the Holy Grail*, Franz Strassen's illustration for Act 3, is replaced by the

Nazi Eagle flying aloft in the propaganda image *Es Lebe Deutschland.* Similarly, *The Standard Bearer* can be likened to popular early-twentieth century imagery of Parsifal, in this case Pogany's depiction of Parsifal.

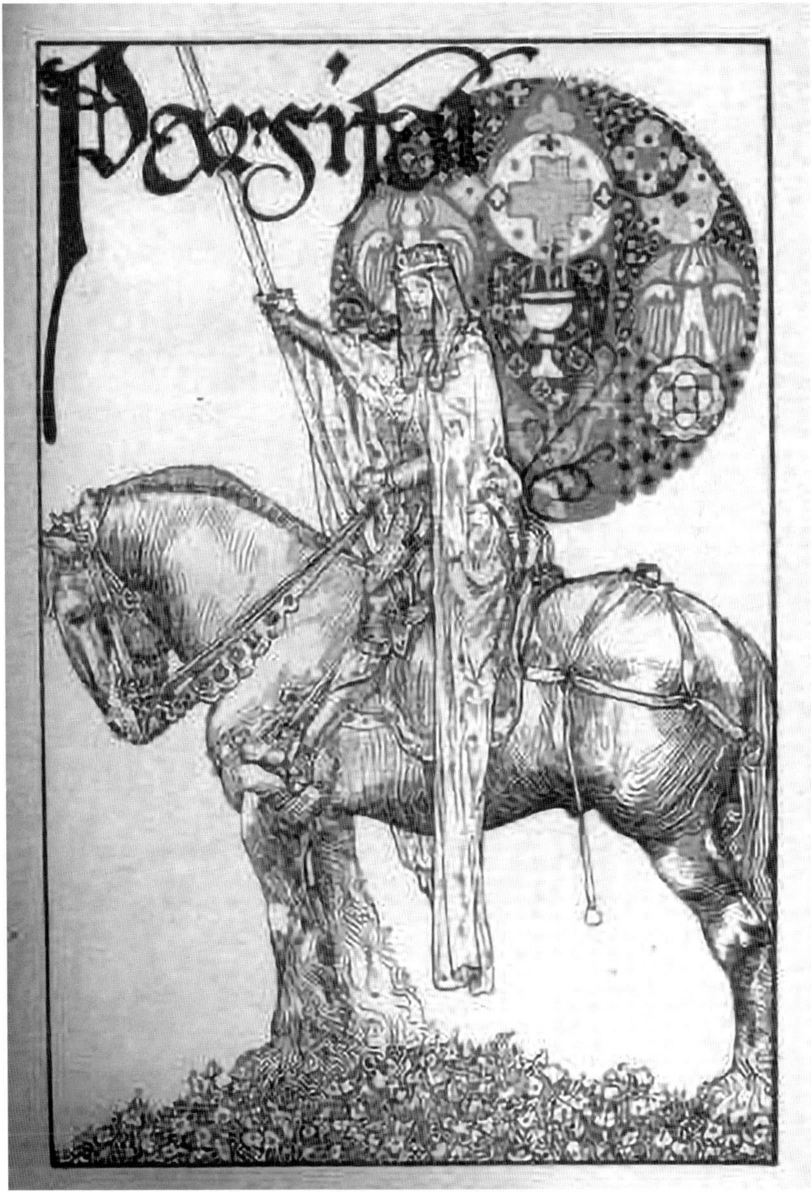

Rolleston, T.W., *Parsifal or the Legend of the Holy Grail retold from Ancient Sources with acknowledgement to the 'Parsifal' of Richard Wagner*, illustrated by Willy Pogany, George G. Harrap & Co., 1912.

The Standard Bearer, painted by Hubert Lanzinger for the Great German Art Exhibition, Munich, 1937.

Es lebe Deutschland (Long live Germany) poster from the 1930s. Designed by K. Stauber.

Chapter 12

The End of Rahn

The capture of the lance perhaps served to highlight the lack of success achieved by Rahn. Himmler had far more of an interest in the occult and mysticism than Hitler. Himmler may have been appeased by Rahn waxing lyrical about the heretical mysticism of the Grail in *The Court of Lucifer*, but Hitler was less impressed, and his patience with Rahn had by now run out.

As we have demonstrated, Hitler's interests in the Grail quest were two-fold, to promote the idea of Germany having ownership of 'positive Christianity' and, more importantly, to bring to reality the legend of Parsifal with Hitler centre stage, playing the role of the hero.

Hitler wanted the Holy Grail, which was the object of his desire. Were the Holy Grail to be reunited with the Holy Lance, he would truly have brought to reality the legend of Parsifal. But to this end, Rahn had failed to keep his part of the bargain.

Rahn had never truly lost faith in the belief that the legend of Parzival held the key to finding the Grail. He had searched high and low; he had explored numerous theories but all to no avail. It was now that he was running out of options.

On 28 February 1939, Rahn submitted a report on St Odilien (St Odile), entitled 'Gral', directly to Himmler. The report detailed another failed attempt to locate the Grail. Rahn had acted on information suggesting that the monastery of St Odilien had been a hiding place for the Grail. St Odilien had sought refuge in the hermitage where Treverizent, Eschenbach's Grail hermit, instructed Parzival. Other than suggesting the bloodline of St Odilien were keepers of the 'secrets of the Grail' Rahn's report revealed nothing of any significance and certainly nothing to suggest he was any closer to finding the Grail. There were no avenues Rahn could see left to explore.

On the same day, Rahn submitted his report to Himmler, he sent a letter to SS-Gruppenführer Wolff:

> *'Gruppenführer! Unfortunately, I have to ask you to ask the Reichsführer SS for my immediate dismissal from the Schutzstaffel. The reasons for that are so deep and serious that I can explain them only orally. For that purpose, I will come to Berlin in the next days and report to you. Heil Hitler, Otto Rahn.'*[1]

It is reported that a few days later Rahn turned up in Dortmund at the flat of Karl Eggers, a fellow Nazi author. Also there was Albert von Haller, a publisher, previously used by Rahn. Both men were known to Rahn. In a distraught state, Rahn confided in them telling them the SS were after him. He had been given a choice between entering a concentration camp or committing suicide in the mountains. Rahn was on the run.

On 8 March, Rahn was in Freiberg and visited his first publisher and friend Otto Vogelsgang, in the Hotel Zahringerhof. Vogelsgang later described Rahn's mood as being calm; it could well be that by this time Rahn had accepted his fate.

Rahn made one further visit, whilst fleeing, to the Lauermann family in Schliersee. Dietmar Lauermann had been a friend of Rahn since 1933, when they both broadcast on a Frankfurt local radio station and socialised on the university campus. During this time, Rahn had spent time at Lauermann family home. This was a farewell visit in which Rahn would say his last goodbye. The Lauermanns, nor any of Rahn's other friends, family or acquaintances, would ever see Rahn alive again.

Dietmar Lauermann later said that Rahn left them on 12 March, making his way through Neuhaus and Kufstein before reaching Soll, where he checked in to a small hotel. The next day, he caught a bus,

Grail Knight Leap of Faith Painting, giclee printed on artist canvas. As seen in *Indiana Jones and the Last Crusade.*

getting off at a stop known as the 'stony path', from there he walked off into the mountains. These were the last known steps of Otto Rahn.

On 17 March, Otto Rahn was dismissed from the SS with a retrospective date of 28 February, the date he resigned. In an about turn, Rahn was readmitted into the SS and on 25 May a notice appeared in *Das Schwarzes Korps*, the newspaper of the SS.

There is much debate about whether Rahn was a true Nazi, but it is undebatable he took the 'Nazi schilling' without hesitation and wore the Nazi uniform. He suffered no worse a death than millions of innocents who died at the hands of the merciless SS, the organisation to which he had sworn allegiance and whose uniform he had worn.

Three months later, on 28 August, the 'Weisthor', Karl Maria Wiligut, who had been Rahn's handler since 1933 when Rahn first came to the attention of the Nazis, was stripped of his commission in the SS.

Map showing significant places in Germany.

On 1 September, Germany invaded Poland; the Second World War had commenced, and the Nazi quest for the Holy Grail had come to an end.

Later that year, on 13 November, a dossier comprising Rahn's research file was sent from Himmler's office to the chief of SS personnel. The final sentence of the dossier reads that 'The decision concerning the former Brigadier Weisthor is pending.'

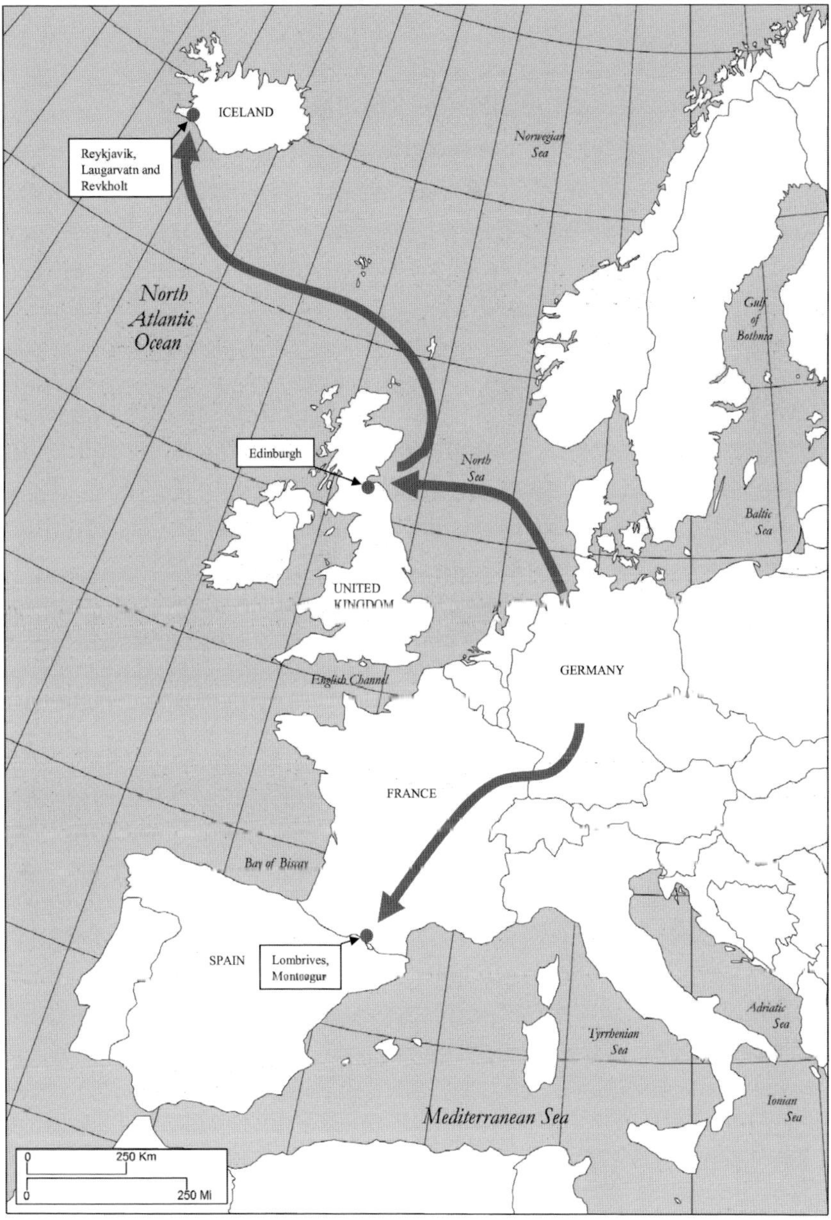

Map of western Europe showing places explored by Rahn as part of the Nazi Grail quest.

'Weisthor' did not suffer the same fate as Rahn and survived the war, but his mental and physical health had declined to such an extent that he died on 3 January 1946 shortly after the war ended.

In visiting Britain, Rahn had come close to finding the truth of the Grail without realising it. He was perhaps beginning to realize that the Grail was not a physical object, but that was not what his masters wanted to hear. What Hitler desired was an object he could hold aloft in his hands, just as Parsifal had done.

An SS obituary published on 18 May 1939 read: 'During a blizzard in the mountains, the SS-Obersturmführer Otto Rahn died tragically. We regret that and lost with him a decent SS member and the creator of marvellous historic and scientific works.' Rahn died with the Grail tantalisingly out of reach.

Part II

Peredur – The Truth of the Grail

'Too many investigators, professional scholars as well as amateurs, in their search for answers to the riddle of the Grail have looked in the most unlikely places, and resemble an absent-minded gentleman who hunts for his pince-nez in the refrigerator, the waste-basket, the medicine cabinet, the pockets of his riding-breeches, and the grandfather clock, while the object of his search is resting on his nose. Would it not be sensible to seek the clues to the mystery of the Grail, not in Mohammedan, or Albigensian, or late Hellenic cults, but in the history of Arthurian romance?'[1]

Roger Sherman Loomis (1991)

Prologue to Part II

Rahn never found Perceval and his death ended the Nazi quest for the Grail. In coming to Britain and exploring the roots of the King Arthur story in the north of Britain, Rahn had come within touching distance of the truth he sought. His preoccupation

King Arthur and the Knights of the Round Table behold a vision of the Holy Grail. Perceval is depicted at the rear to the right of centre.

with the Cathars clouded his judgement though. He left Britain having explored Arthur's Seat in Edinburgh, without delving deeper into the roots of the legend that would have brought him to the truth behind the Grail stories.

The Parzival story upon which Rahn based his whole search for the Grail was derived from the stories of King Arthur and the Knights of the Round Table, specifically, the story of Sir Perceval. Rahn touched upon this without uncovering the origins of these stories, key to unlocking the mystery of the Grail.

The underpinning truth that Rahn never reached was that the legend of Perceval was founded upon the life of a Yorkshire knight of the Dark Ages, Peredur.

The stories of King Arthur and the Knights of the Round Table, upon which Rahn pinned his hopes of finding the Grail on, were written in the Middle Ages and given a contemporary setting, a setting consistent in time with the crusades. Knowledge of the characters later portrayed as the Knights of the Round Table had grown and spread to continental Europe with the writing of Geoffrey of Monmouth, who in 1136 completed his *The History of the Kings of Britain*, a pseudohistory of the British people akin to a 'Marvel' collection of superhero tales. Almost all the characters and events portrayed in Monmouth's work, though, have a factual basis. It is just that his flamboyant use of language and imaginative approach to filling in details he is unsure of mean he is a less reliable source than some other chroniclers, who, on the flip side, offer less detail than Monmouth. Monmouth's work coincided with similar, if not identical, tales of British heroes being circulated around the courts of England and France by Breton, British (Welsh) and Anglo-Norman bards. These tales reverberated in the 'bruts', literary works equivalent to movie remakes of Monmouth's work, produced by Wace, Layamon and others. It was in this context that the great Arthurian Romances were spawned.

Rahn either remained largely ignorant of or discounted the fact that these tales, the stories of Parzival and Perceval in particular, were not rooted in the crusading period of the high Middle Ages, an age of chivalry and knights in shining armour; they stemmed from a much earlier time, the Dark Ages, the time from the fifth century onwards when Roman 'civilisation' capitulated, so called because of the lack of writing to shed light on the era. A time when Roman influence in Britain had collapsed, and the native British were being driven from their homelands by the Saxons invading from the east.

In the fifth and sixth centuries, the British were fighting for survival, as more and more land-grabbing Saxons came to their shores. Inevitably, conflict resulted. The heroes of the Britons wars with the Saxons were celebrated in legend. It was in these wars that the legend of King Arthur was born. Stories from this time survived as oral traditions and as such were passed down from generation to generation.

During the Dark Ages, the native British were hounded out of large parts of what we now call England by the Saxons and took refuge in the hills of what is now Wales and Cornwall in the west. Some escaped over the sea to the place that took their name in France – Brittany. It is in these places that their stories and culture have been preserved to this day. A result of this migration is that many of the heroes of Welsh and Cornish culture in fact lived out their lives in northern England or the Midlands. It may well be that King Arthur himself was in fact a northern chieftain based in Yorkshire. What is a sure bet is that the legend of Sir Percival, Parzival in German culture, was based on the life of Peredur, the son of a sixth-century British king, based in York.

It would be many years before the story of these legends passed into writing. One such story, *Peredur the Son of Evrawc*, found its way into *The Mabinogion*, a collection of eleven medieval Welsh folk tales translated into English in the mid-nineteenth century by Lady Charlotte Guest. Although much older in origin, the story of *Peredur the Son of Evrawc*, is preserved in written form in both sources of Guest's *The Mabinogion*, the *White Book of Rhydderch* (1300–25) and the *Red Book of Hergest* (1375–1425). However, the earliest written extant version of the story is likely to be Peniarth MS 7, a manuscript held in the National Library of Wales.

Peredur the Son of Evrawc, is almost certainly the foundation for Chrétien de Troyes's *Perceval*; the story where the first mention of the Grail occurs. Chrétien tells us that Perceval, the hero of his romance, is an aspirant young Welshman. The inspiration for Chrétien's romances were the Brythonic tales of Celtic gods and heroes he heard relayed by Breton bards entertaining their hosts in the court of Champagne. These bards were descendants of Britons, who had escaped from the tyranny of the Saxons in Britain in the sixth century.

Peredur the Son of Evrawc, is similar in content to Chrétien de Troyes's *Perceval*, and there has been some conjecture about which of the two stories preceded the other. However, *Peredur the son of Evrawc* bears all the hallmarks of Dark Age, British tradition, the culture from which Peredur heralded, whereas *Perceval* is an adaptation of the original story, removed from the British origins of the story with events transposed into a continental setting and characters bearing continental names.

This is the truth that Rahn never discovered. He found it difficult to shift focus and move away from his theory that the Grail legend was spawned in the heroic acts of the Cathars in escaping the persecution of the Albigensian Crusade. The time when the stories were written, from the twelfth century onwards, is not when the stories came into being.

It was *Peredur the Son of Evrawc*, not Raimon Roger Trenceval, the Cathar hero and central focus of Rahn's search, who was the original inspiration for the character of Perceval and consequently Parzival. It is, therefore, *Peredur the Son of Evrawc* who will lead us to the truth Rahn sought but failed to find in taking *Perceval* as being an original source.

Chapter 13

The *Mabinogion*

The story of *Peredur the Son of Evrawc*, is one of the three Welsh romances associated with *The Mabinogion*. The eleven Welsh folk tales, translated by Lady Charlotte Guest, were first published as *The Mabinogion* in 1840. The title of Guest's work comes from the Welsh word *mabinogion*, meaning tale of a hero's boyhood. Guest mistakenly used the term 'Mabinogion' as the plural of this.

The tales Guest translated are taken from the *White Book of Rhydderch* and the *Red Book of Hergest*. Although the *White Book of Rhydderch* was compiled in the early-fourteenth century and the *Red Book of Hergest* in the years either side of 1400, parts of these tales were written as early as the second half of the eleventh century. Some of the stories are much older still, stemming from oral traditions passed down from generation to generation through the first millennium.

This compares with Chrétien de Troyes's *Perceval* written c.1180 and Wolfram von Eschenbach's *Parzival*, completed c.1210.

Given that *Peredur the Son of Evrawc*, *Perceval* and *Parzival* are similar stories based in the court of King Arthur, what is most likely is that they all emanate from British oral traditions relating to Peredur, a known historical character from the Arthurian period.

Whilst in the court of Philippe of Alsace, Count of Flanders, Chrétien would have listened to Breton storytellers, descendants of Britons who fled the island for Armorica, the province of France now known as Brittany, to escape the devastation and slaughter brought to Britain by the Saxon invaders. These storytellers would know tales about Arthur and other British heroes who had fought against the Saxons.

It is through these Breton bards that Chrétien would have heard tell of Peredur and his association with the Grail. He then rewrote the tale in a manner to suit his patron, and so Peredur became Perceval who became Parzival.

Chapter 14

The Grail Story

The three principal versions of the Grail story we have considered are:

Peredur AD 1100–1200
Perceval AD 1178–91
Parzival AD 1209–15

All three stories contain a common basic theme with the elements outlined below.

A life-giving and sustenance dispensing object is guarded in a hidden-away castle by a king. The king is either crippled or sick, and the land surrounding the castle is laid to waste. The only way that the king can regain his health is if a knight of obvious merit finds his way to the castle and on seeing the object asks a certain question. If the knight fails to ask the correct question, the unfortunate situation of the king's health and the barrenness of the land surrounding the castle remains unremedied. The castle then disappears, and the knight sets out in search of it once again. By way of many adventures, the knight refinds the Grail Castle, and this time asks the correct question. The king's health is thus restored, and the land returned to plentifulness. The knight becomes a hero and guardian of the Grail from that time on.

The stories differ in their settings and how different elements of the theme outlined above are dealt with.

Chapter 15

The Historical Peredur

Peredur was born into a royal line, the kings of northern Britain, whose seat lay in York (Evrawc). In Roman times, York was named Eboracum. When Britain was abandoned by Rome, in the early part of the fourth century AD, York remained a place of regional governance and a hub of commercial activity. Local tribal leaders simply took the place of Roman officials. Eboracum, the Roman name for York, was corrupted to Evrawc by the British, before becoming Eoforwick under the Saxons, Jorvik under the Vikings and then eventually York as we know it today.

Peredur was a descendant of Coel Hen, who famously passed into history as 'Old King Cole', he of the 'merry old soul'. Although Coel became the stuff of nursery rhymes, he was in fact a northern chieftain of great repute in the Dark Ages.

Few dates in the Dark Ages can be nailed down with any conviction; scant evidence exists, and differing chronologies are common. What we can say with confidence, by piecing together clues given in medieval manuscripts, is that Peredur was born sometime in the mid-sixth century. A time perhaps when Arthur was a pre-eminent ruler. A time when, although Saxons remained settled on the island of Britain, the British wars with the Saxons had ceased.

Coel Hen, from whom Peredur was descended, had ruled over a kingdom encompassing the whole of the north, south of Hadrian's Wall. Following his death, Coel's kingdom was partitioned and shared among his descendants, with what had been the capital, York, passing to Peredur's father Eleuther. Eleuther has been referred to as Eleuther 'of the Great Army' by Morris in *The Age of Arthur*.[1] This suggests

Peredur's father had been a key part of the British coalition force that had secured a decisive victory over the Saxons at Mount Badon.

The invading Saxons had brought tyranny to Britain, but their incursions had been arrested by Ambrosius Aurelanius around 466 and brought to a halt by the British victory at Badon of c.495, a victory attributed by the Welsh bard Nennius to Arthur, later known as 'King Arthur'. Arthur's glorious victory at Badon is also recorded in the *Annales Cambraie* (Annals of Wales): 'The Battle of Badon, in which Arthur carried the Cross of our Lord Jesus Christ for three days and three nights on his shoulders and the Britons were the victors.'

Elsewhere in medieval Welsh literature, Peredur is referred to as 'Long Spear' or 'Steel Spear'. An explanation of this appendage to Peredur's name is offered by *Y Seint Greal*, a Welsh romance commissioned by the noble Hopcyn ap Thomas of Glamorgan in the latter years of the fourteenth century:

> '*His name is Peredur.... For the reason that when the boy was born his father caused him to be given this name 'Steel Spear' because the Lord of the Fens was waging war on Evrawc. Therefore, the boy was called Peredur, so that when he should be a grown man, he should be mindful of. Or else, by the might of a steel spear he should avenge the Lord of the Fens what he had done to his father in taking his lands from him.*'[2]

These days, we think of the 'Fens' as being the flat fenlands of East Anglia, however, this has not always been the case; prior to the seventeenth century, extensive tracts of wetland north of East Anglia still existed. The Humber basin was awash with wetlands stretching from South Yorkshire to the Vale of York in the north and east through Pickering and Holderness.

The 'Lord of the Fens' referred to was in all probability an early leader of the Angles who had settled in the then wetlands of the Vale of York. These people would become part of the Anglo-Saxon kingdom

Illustration by Willy Pogany from *Parsifal or the Legend of the Holy Grail retold from Ancient Sources with acknowledgement to the 'Parsifal' of Richard Wagner* by T.W. Rolleston, George G. Harrap & Co., 1912.

of Deira, which extended from the Humber in the south to the Tees in the north. Eventually, Deira expanded westwards to envelope the city of York and the village of Catterick, but at the time of Peredur's birth, Deira was if anything a fledgling kingdom, made up of Angles who had settled in the land once held by the native Britons known as the Parisi, who had held sway in East Yorkshire. This territory just encroached on the eastern outskirts of York.

It is plausible then that the Deirans took lands from Peredur's father, Eleuther, whose powerbase lay in York. The first recorded leader of the Deirans was Aelle, ruling in 597, probably some fifty years after the birth of Peredur. However, a man named Yffi is listed in the *Anglo-Saxon Chronicle* as being his father and who may well have been the leader of the Deirans prior to this time.

However, following the British victory over the Saxons at Badon, civil troubles became the preoccupation of the British kings. According to Gildas, a contemporary ecclesiastical writer, these troubles were the result of 'the wickedness of those who are become servants, not only to their bellies, but also to the devil rather than to Christ'.

The very process that afforded Peredur a regal inheritance was also a key factor in bringing about these fractious times. Unlike in later medieval times, when following the death of a king, his realm passed to his eldest son and heir, the death of a king in the Dark Ages resulted in his kingdom being partitioned among all his sons and daughters. This led to wrestling for power becoming commonplace among siblings. Thus, an uneasy alliance existed among the descendants of Coel Hen.

It was in these civil troubles that the young Peredur, who perhaps because of his prowess in fighting was known as Peredur 'Steel Arms' or 'Steal Spear' (*The Book of Aneirin*), became embroiled. It is likely this unrest was a product of some kings slipping from Christianity into the pagan beliefs and practices of the ancient British. This is supported not only by Gildas's castigation of all but a 'very few' native citizens inhabiting the island at this time, but also by what we can glean from the Welsh romances, which speak of magic, sorcery and witchcraft occurring in or about royal courts.

If we are to believe what we are told in *Peredur the Son of Evrawc*, Peredur was the seventh of seven sons of the Earl of Evrawc, who we can assume to be Eleuther. Accounts vary, but according to said romance, Peredur was left alone with his mother after his father and six elder brothers perished in battle. This is a recurring theme in Arthurian tales, with both Ambrosius and King Arthur being portrayed by writers of the Middle Ages as having been fatherless through childhood. So, it is likely some artistic license was employed here by the anonymous author of 'Peredur', a work which is, after all, a romance.

We can turn here to the *Black Book of Carmarthen*, which is believed to be written by a single scholar about 1250 and deemed to be one of 'Four Ancient Books of Wales' by William Forbes Skene (1809–92). The book is a collection of poems referring to times past and is of particular interest in that it contains poems set in the 'Old North' and ones connected with the legends of Arthur and Myrddin, or Merlin. One of the poems in the *Black Book of Carmarthen* is entitled 'Ymddiddan Myrddin a Thaliesin' ('A Conversation Between Merlin and Taliesin'). In this poem, Myrddin (Merlin) tells Taliesin that Eleuther, the Earl of Evrawc, had seven sons, and that all seven sons fought together at the Battle of P.

Opposing them in the battle was an army led by Gwenduleu, another northern ruler descended from Coel Hen, who held sway in the Carlisle region.

It has been asserted that the Battle of Ardderyd, now Arthuret, ten miles north of Carlisle, was among the two most significant battles of the Dark Ages. Whatever, it was no small affair according to Skene, with bardic traditions alleging the field was attended by no less than 80,000 Britons.

Snippets of information can also be gleaned from the Welsh Triads. The Triads are a brand of poetry unique to Welsh medieval manuscripts in which groups of three objects are referred to under a heading indicating a common likeness. In doing this, the Triads offer a medieval Welsh perspective of events in what has been termed the 'British Heroic Age' of the sixth and seventh centuries. The Triad of 'Three Horses who carried Three Horse-Burdens' suggests the sons of Eliffer were aided in the battle by 'Dunawt the Stout', who we can equate to Dunawt of the Pennines and 'Cynfelyn the Leprous', which corroborates the idea put forward by Morris that a federation of forces from the Yorkshire region banded together to fight against Gwendoleu at Ardderyd. Dunawt is also named in one of the Triads as being one of the 'Three Pillars of Battle on the Island of Britain': 'Corvan, horse of the sons of Eliffer, bore the second Horse-Burden: he carried on his back Gwrgi and Peredur and Dunawd the Stout and Cynfelyn the Leprous(?), to look upon the battle-fog of (the host of) Gwenddolau (in) Ar(f)derydd.'[3]

The *Annales Cambriae* give a date for the battle of 573 and offer further detail: 'The Battle of Ardderyd between the sons of Eliffer and Gwendoleu the son of Ceidio; in which battle Gwendoleu fell; Merlin became mad.'

We can cross reference the result of the battle with a stanza contained in the *Red Book of Hergest*: 'As Gwendoleu was slain in the blood-spilling of Ardderyd.'

All accounts are consistent in suggesting the battle was a tumultuous affair with no shortage of ferocity likely stoked by mead. Merlin, or Myrddin, was the bard of Gwendoleu, and the defeat and slaughter of his leader and kinsmen was clearly a devastating event.

'Yr Afallenau', or Sweet Appletree, is a post-Ardderyd lament by Merlin in which he expresses his grief at the outcome of the battle and the death of Gwendoleu. It also suggests he may have fought in the battle:

> *'I am hated by the firmest minister of Rydderch;*
> *For after Gwendolleu no princes honour me;*
> *I am not soothed with diversion, I am not visited by the fair;*
> *Yet in the battle of Ardderyd, golden was my torques.'*[4]

Earlier lines from the lament suggest that after the battle Merlin hid out in the woods of Celyddon (Caledonian Forest) nearby:

> *'When, with my shield on my shoulder, and my sword on my thigh,*
> *I slept all alone in the woods of Celyddon.'*[5]

Merlin's legacy is commemorated by a cave named after him high on Hart Fell. In Merlin's time, a hillside covered in dense forest. It was perhaps here that Merlin sought refuge after the battle.

Control of Gwendoleu's kingdom was passed to Rhydderch, a powerful king ruling at Strathclyde, and it is clear from passages in Merlin's lament that he did not enjoy the same cordial relationship with the leaders of the new administration as he had done with Gwendoleu.

It has long been suggested that the principal motivations for the battle were religious. Skene puts forward the idea that 'a struggle seems to have taken place between Christian and pagan elements in the country' at this time and that Ardderyd was 'the true field of the contest between the Christian and semi-pagan chiefs'. Going back over a century, Christianity become widespread among the Romano-British after being adopted by Constantine the Great, the man who had been proclaimed emperor at York in AD 306. Christianity became popular in the Romanised townships of Britain, with York being proclaimed a bishopric in AD 314, whilst paganism held sway in barren regions that clung to the native culture, including the mountains of Scotland, which were never tamed by the Romans.

Gwendoleu held sway in the hills of southern Scotland, ruling over his people from a stronghold at the confluence of the rivers Esk and Liddel; a domain where paganism is likely to have flourished. Nikolai Tolstoy, the celebrated, quasi-Russian Celtic historian, strongly argues there is an abundance of evidence indicating that Gwendoleu was a strong believer in and indeed a defender of ancient British pagan traditions. He was one of the three 'Bull Protectors of Britain', which was an esteemed ceremonial position in pagan Celtic society. The

Welsh Triads offer another clear clue as to the paganism practised by Gwendoleu and his followers who slew the 'Two Birds of Gwendoleu', saying 'And they had a yoke of gold. Two corpses of the Britons they ate for their supper'. Pairs of birds similarly harnessed by gold or silver are prevalent in Irish pagan verses. Contained within this verse, there is also a strong hint of human sacrifice. A separate avine reference contained in the *Black Book of Carmarthen* speaks of a supernatural goose attacking Gwallawg, who was a cousin of Gwendoleu:

> *'Cursed be the white goose*
> *Which tore the eye from the head*
> *Of Gwallawg ab Lleenawg.'*[6]

The goose possessed divine attributes for the Celts and may well have been seen as a harbinger of the afterworld. This is suggested by a Pictish carving at Aberlemno in Angus depicting a predatory fowl pecking at the face of a falling warrior.

Further evidence of the pagan outlook of Gwendoleu is provided in yet another Triad that talks of Gwendoleu possessing a magical chess set 'if the pieces were set, they would play by themselves. The board was of gold and the men of silver.'

If we accept the chess pieces and geese or swans cited by Tolstoy as being evidence of a pagan culture, we must also reflect on the fact that another tale, contained in the *Red Book of Hergest*, makes reference to King Arthur himself being involved in a plot containing supernatural geese capable of slaying men, a magical carpet that rendered him invisible and also a chess set with magical powers. Indeed, there are even magical chess pieces and pagan rituals evident in tales of Peredur himself, although perhaps crucially, Peredur does not have ownership of the chess pieces. It may be that such magical accompaniments were simply a device to 'spice' up stories, rather than being indicative of characters having dabbled in the paranormal. It is also likely; some British kings hedged their bets by having a foot in both camps.

Myrddin, or Merlin, advisor of Gwendoleu, was clearly pagan, perhaps one of the last of druids or Celtic shaman. This accounts for the uneasy relationship he had with Rhydderch, who was a champion of Christianity, and his administrators after control of what had been Gwendoleu's kingdom, passed to them.

On balance, it seems likely that Gwendoleu at least had leanings towards paganism if not a key figure in the native religion with him having been one of the 'Bull Protectors of Britain'.

It should be noted that Merlin as written about in Arthurian tales of the Middle Ages was a conglomerative character created by Geoffrey of Monmouth, who merged tales of Myrddin with those of the young Ambrose by the Welsh bard Nennius to create the character of Merlin that suited his purposes.

There is much reason to believe that Peredur, in contrast to Gwendoleu, was a Christian. Christianity had been widely adopted in the Roman townships of Britain by the end of the century; it was only in rural districts that paganism remained. When the remaining Roman legions left Britain to defend continental interests in the dying days of the empire, Christianity had become ensconced in urban society. York was likely a hub of the faith; the city was a bishopric in the fourth century, and when Pope Gregory sent a mission to Britain in 601, he selected York to be the church's centre in the north.

Following the tumultuous Battle of Ardderyd, where Gwendoleu was defeated and killed by his cousins, who were the kings or princes of York, Peredur, it seems, returned to York triumphant.

There are no wars recorded between the British of Evrawc, or York, and the Deirans, who were the Angles or English settled in the Yorkshire Wolds in the sixth century. It seems likely the two peoples lived alongside each other relatively peaceably. This is attested to by the similarity between the cremation pottery of this period from the York cemeteries and those of the Wolds, which show that the two possessed close cultural affinities.[7]

However, it wasn't long before more trouble was afoot for Peredur. The former British kingdom of Bernicia had passed into the hands of the Angles led by Ida, who established his stronghold at Bamburgh and posed a threat to the northern border of the British kingdom of York. Ida is said to have conquered the north, and the Bernicians may well have been intent on further expansion of their kingdom under the leadership of Adda, who succeeded his father as king. Peredur, who now ruled York along with his brother Gurci, felt compelled to march north to counter the growing threat, but the brothers were defeated and killed by Adda at Caer Greu in 580. Their defeat was decisive, and the British kingdom of York, which had been the most important of the British northern states, ended with their death. According to Morris, with Peredur's army dispersed, the Deirans led by Aelle, or his father, occupied the city of York.

It is interesting to note what one of the Triads, 'Three Faithless War-Bands of the Islands of Britain' has to say about the deaths of Peredur and Gurci:

> *'The War-Band of Goronwy the Radiant of (Penllyn), who refused to receive the poisoned spear from Lleu Skilful-Hand on behalf of their lord, at the Stone of Goronwy at the head of the Cynfal; and the War-Band of Gwrgi and Peredur, who abandoned their lord at Caer Greu, when they had an appointment to fight the next day with Eda Great-Knee; and there they were both slain; And the War-Band of Alan Fyrgan, who turned away from him by night, and let him go with his servants to Camlan. And there he was slain.'*[8]

It has been suggested that the slayer, Eda the Great Knee, is equivalent to Ida. Chronologies make this unlikely, but it is likely derived from the knowledge that it was the Bernicians who were responsible for the deaths of the brothers, and Eda, being a corruption of Adda, fits the bill. It is likely the Britons under the command of the brothers were significantly outnumbered and widespread fear led to large proportion of them deserting the field, leaving Peredur and Gurci to their fate.

Another of the Welsh Triads, 'Three Prostrate Chieftains of the Island of Britain', alludes to Peredur leaving a son, who would find any reconquest of York beyond his powers.

> *'Llywarch the Old son of Elidir Llydanwyn, and Manawydan son of Llyr Half-Speech, and Gwgon Gwron son of Peredur son of Eliffer of the Great Retinue. And this is why those were called "Prostrate Chieftains": because they would not seek a dominion, which nobody could deny it to them.'*[9]

After the fall of York, British influence in Yorkshire was maintained in the kingdom of Elmet until c.617. At this time, the men of Elmet were defeated in battle, having been pushed near Bawtry by Edwin, who was king of the newly formed Northumbria.

An anomaly to the history of Peredur as we have set it out is a passage contained in 'Y Gododdin', a poem from the *Book of Aneirin*:

> *'The men went to Catraeth fed with mead and drunk.*
> *Their life was the price of their banquet of mead: –*
> *Caradawg and Madawg, Pyll and Ieuan,*
> *Gwgawn and Gwiawn, Gwyn and Cynvan,*
> *Peredur with steel arms, Gwawrddur and Aeddan*
> *A defence were they in the tumult, though with shattered shields,*
> *When they were slain, they also slaughtered;*
> *Not one to his native home returned.'*

The poem is an ode to the brave men of the north who died at the battle of Catraeth, and Peredur is clearly counted as being among their number. Morris gives a date of 598 for the Battle of Catraeth, which he refers to as the 'annals'. This is eighteen years after the date of Peredur's death in 580 according to the *Annales Cambriae*. Caer Greu, on initial inspection, is incongruous with Catraeth. It is important to remember none of these dates are cast in stone and, therefore, there are several possibilities:

1. There is more than one Peredur. This seems unlikely as all genealogies refer to Peredur being the son of Eleuther.
2. Catraeth and Caer Greu are the same place, possible, but again unlikely; the graphemes contained in each of the place names are quite different and both appear to be British place names. Catraeth is thought to be Catterick, while the site of Caer Greu us unidentified.
3. The battles of Caer Greu and Catraeth were fought against the same enemy (the Bernicians or Northumbrians) and not too far apart either geographically or chronologically. Aneirin may simply have clumped them both together and gone with the name of the bigger battle Catraeth in his ode.

The third possibility seems the most likely to my mind. It is believed Aneirin was a survivor of the Battle of Catraeth and perhaps employed a degree of poetic licence in naming Catraeth as the site of the last stand of Peredur and his 'band of brothers'.

This is what we can reasonably ascertain about the life of the historical Peredur, who undoubtedly existed. Our task now is to see how if in any way the story of *Peredur the Son of Evrawc* relates to the real life of the historical Peredur.

Chapter 16

Peredur the Son of Evrawc (A Tale from *The Mabinogion*)

As highlighted in Chapter 14, the three principal versions of the Grail story we have considered are:

Peredur AD 1100–1200
Perceval AD 1178–91
Parzival AD 1209–15

The dates given for each of these versions of the Grail story are generally accepted as being when they were written. All these stories contain a common basic theme with the elements outlined below. The young P (Peredur/Perceval/Parzival) is raised alone in the woods by his mother away from courtly society after his father is killed in combat. As P begins to come of age, by chance he meets a small band of knights in the woods and leaving his mother, he goes with them to the court of King Arthur. P encounters a young maiden in a tent and takes from her an item of jewellery. This leads to unrest between the maiden and her husband when he returns. At the court of King Arthur, P is mocked by Kay and takes up a challenge to fight another knight. P wins the fight and avails the knight of his armour and horse. P rides away to a castle where he is given instruction on armed combat and knightly conduct by a friendly lord. P enters a second castle where he is presented with a magical sword, and the Grail, along with a bloody lance, are paraded before him.

The stories differ in their settings and how different elements of the theme outlined above are dealt with. A comparison of the common elements in each story is provided in Appendix I.

Our task now is to compare the story of *Peredur the Son of Evrawc*, with what we know of the life of the historical Peredur. In the first instance, the family background we are given for Peredur is consistent with what we are told in the *Black Book of Carmarthen* and corroborated by other sources including the Triads and the *Annales Cambriae* as discussed earlier.

We are also told in the story that 'Evrawc maintained himself not so much by his own possessions as by attending tournaments, and wars, and combats.' It has been presupposed that references in the Welsh romances to tournaments were the result of medieval influences, however, there is plenty of archaeological evidence to strongly suggest cavalry tournaments (*hippika gymnasia*) took place in Britain during Roman times. We know Roman cavalry units stationed in Britain took part in tournaments, and there is every reason to believe that British warriors of what is often referred to as the Heroic Age, who continued to fight on horseback armed with helmet, armour, sword and spear, also continued the tradition of tournaments, unlike the Saxons who fought on foot.

In Roman times, these tournaments were grand affairs that were very much in keeping with later medieval tournaments. We know about Roman tournaments from the writings of Arrian, who was commissioned by Emperor Hadrian to produce a military manual, the *Ars Tactica.* The following passage, taken from the *Ars Tactica*, provides details of such tournaments:

> *'The horsemen enter [the parade ground] fully armed, and those of high rank or superior in horsemanship wear gilded helmets of iron or bronze to draw the attention of the spectators. Unlike the helmets made for active service, these do not cover the head and cheeks only but are made to fit all round the faces of the riders with apertures for the eyes ... From the helmets hang yellow plumes, a matter of décor as much as utility. As the horses move forward, the slightest breeze adds to the beauty of these plumes. They carry oblong shields of a lighter type*

> *than those used in action, since both agility and smart turnout are the objects of the exercise, and they improve the appearance of their shields by embellishment. Instead of breastplates the horsemen wear close-fitting Cimmerian tunics [leather jerkins] embroidered with scarlet, red or blue and other colours. On their legs they wear tight trousers, not loosely fitting like those of the Parthians and Armenians. The horses have frontlets carefully made to measure and also have side armour.*'[1]

Arrian also describes events such as jousting with javelins and mock battles, akin to events in medieval tournaments. These events have been successfully tested by experimental archaeologists, who re-enacted the part of Roman cavalrymen.

There have been several finds in Britain of Roman cavalry 'sports helmets', made for cavalrymen competing in *hippika gymnasia*, as well as Roman horse armour designed for tournaments. Interestingly, these helmets, including one found at Guisborough in Yorkshire, were predominantly found away from garrison sites, suggesting their continued use by private individuals not necessarily connected with the Roman army. Furthermore, all the helmets were found in the region of Yr Hen Ogledd (the Old North), the region we now call northern England and the southern Scottish Lowlands, inhabited by Britons in the sub-Roman period and early Middle Ages. The region in which Peredur was born and lived out his life.

We can assume Evrawc, the titular father of Peredur, to be one and the same as Eleuther. Evrawc, the name by which he is referred to in the romance is a version of the name of his domain, Ebrauc, the British name for York, which is derived from its Roman name of Eboracum. It is entirely possible as we have demonstrated that Evrawc 'maintained himself … by attending tournaments, and wars, and combats' as we are told in the story.

According to the tale, Evrawc, also known as Eleuther, dies in battle when Peredur is young. From then on, Peredur is raised by his mother away from inhabited areas in the wilderness of the woods. These can

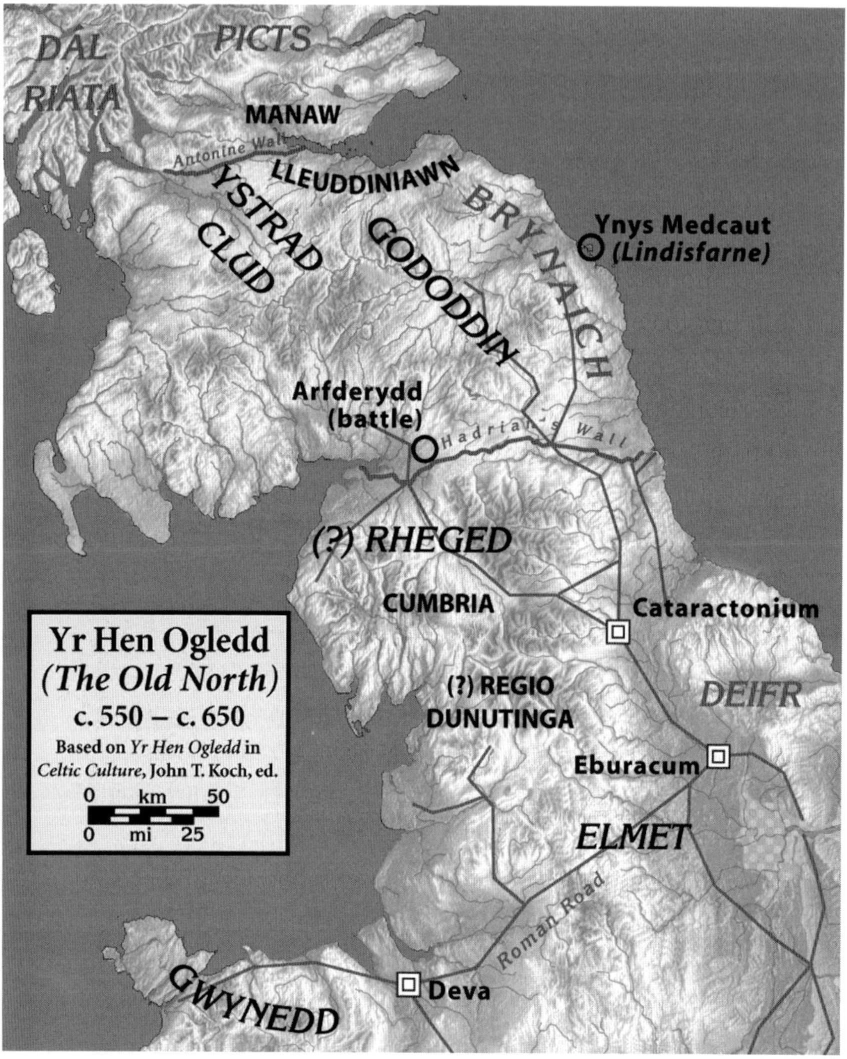

Yr Hen Ogledd (The Old North) c.550–c.650, based on *Yr Hen Ogledd in Celtic Culture*, John T. Koch (ed). (*CC BY-SA 3.0*)

only have been the woods of Elmet located to the south and west; to the east lay the territories of the Angles of Deira and to the north were the warlike Bernicians, who may well have killed Peredur's father, Eleuther.

One day, a band of three knights come to them in search of 'the knight who divided the apples'. The names of the knights were Gwalchmai (Gawain), who was the son of Gwyar, Geneir Gwystyl and Owain, who was the son of Urien Rheged.

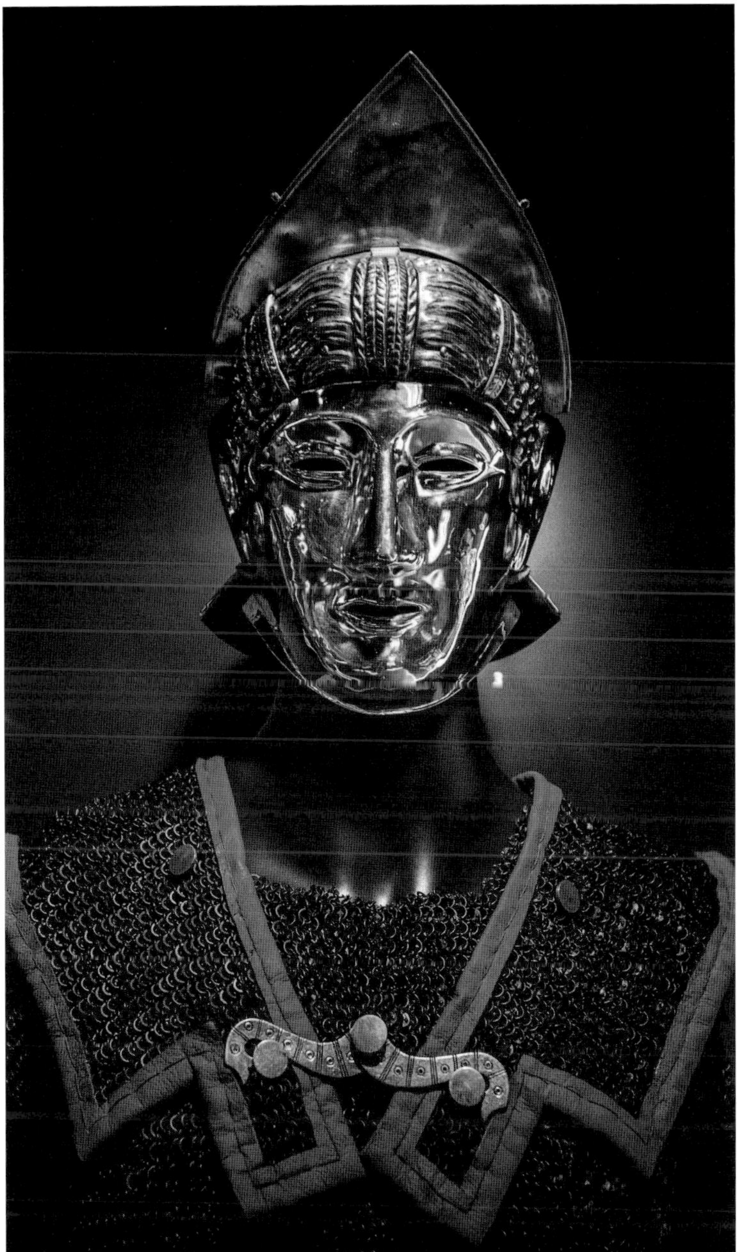

A replica of the Newstead Helmet, an iron Roman cavalry 'sports helmet, dating to AD 80–100 that was discovered in Newstead, near Melrose, in Roxburghshire, Scotland, in 1905. Its discoverer, Sir James Curle (1862–1944), described the helmet as 'one of the most beautiful things that the receding tide of Roman conquest has left behind'.

A lone knight demonstrating his skills during the re-enactment at Carnuntum, Austria, 2008. (*Matthias Kabel*)

Experimental archaeology, re-enacting the *hippika gymnasia* at Carnuntum, Austria, 2008. (*Adsek*)

'The knight who divided the apples' may well be a cryptic reference to the knights being in pursuit of Merlin, the bard of Gwendoleu. Merlin was the author of 'Yr Afallenau', or Sweet Appletree, the lament containing ten stanzas beginning with the words 'Sweet apple tree'.

Geoffrey of Monmouth paraphrases Merlin or Myrddin's words in his 'Vita Merlini' or 'The Life of Merlin':

> *'Christ, God of heaven, what shall I do? In what part of the world can I stay, since I see nothing here, I can live on, neither grass on the ground nor acorns on the trees? Here once there stood nineteen apple trees bearing apples every year; now they are not standing. Who has taken them away from me? Whither have they gone all of a sudden? Now I see them – now I do not! Thus, the fates fight against me and for me, since they both permit and forbid me to see. Now I lack the apples and everything else. The trees stand without leaves, without fruit; I am afflicted by both circumstances since I cannot cover myself with the leaves or eat the fruit. Winter and the south wind with its falling rain have taken them all away.'*[2]

Owain too was a descendant of Coel Hen, but more pertinently, he was a cousin of Peredur on his mother's side. Gwalchmai in later Arthurian literature appears as Gawain, most notably in 'Sir Gawain and the Green Knight'. In another of the romances, 'Owain, or the Lady of the Fountain', Gwalchmai is described as the nephew of Arthur. Gwalchmai is linked to Peredur in the following Triad:

> *'Three Fearless Men of the Island of Britain:*
> *The first was Gwalchmai son of Gwyar,*
> *the second was Llachau son of Arthur,*
> *and the third was (Peredur) son of Earl Efrog.'*[3]

What we can take from this Triad is that both Peredur and Gwalchmai were a generation younger than Arthur. It could also possibly be inferred they were known to him.

The last of the three knights, Geneir Gwystyl, I have been unable to find any further reference to. It could be argued this gives weight to the credulity of the story; why add in the name of an otherwise unheard of knight to make up the band of three?

As the story continues, Peredur goes with the three knights to the court of King Arthur. Much speculation has been undertaken as to which historical figure gave birth to the legend of King Arthur, but two candidates are of particular interest to us here.

Firstly, a northern British king named Arthwys ap Mor. Although genealogies place him a generation before King Arthur's traditionally accepted peers, he was born in the line of Coel Hen and held sway over a large kingdom in the Pennines.

Another northern British candidate for King Arthur is Arthwys, son of Masgwid Gloff, a king to the post-Roman Britons of the Elmet region. This Arthwys fits exactly into the time slot traditionally associated with King Arthur's rule.

According to the story, the young Peredur journeyed two days and two nights in the woody wildernesses and deserted places before he reached the court of Arthur.

Travel on horseback in medieval times, with no spare horse, has been reasonably estimated at 19–25 miles a day. This puts the court of Arthur within 50 miles of the woods just to the west of York where the young Peredur was raised by his mother in the story. Both these candidates for King Arthur fit neatly into this geographical scenario.

It is important to bear in mind at this point that dates in Dark Age Britain are very difficult if not impossible to pinpoint with absolute confidence. Nevertheless, according to accepted chronologies, all the characters named so far in the story are broadly contemporary with each other.

Upon his arrival at the court of Arthur, Peredur is ridiculed by the knight Cei (who in later versions of the story becomes Sir Kay, a knight of the Round Table).

Cei is mentioned as being a warrior in the service of Arthur elsewhere in Welsh literature dating from the eleventh and twelfth centuries, predating Geoffrey of Monmouth's work and Chrétien's *Perceval.*

The earliest of these sources is 'Pa Gur yv y Porthaur' a tenth-century poem from the *Black Book of Carmarthen* in which Arthur gives an account of Cei regarding his prowess in fighting:

> *'Prince of the plunder, / The unrelenting warrior to his enemy; /*
> *Heavy was he in his vengeance; / Terrible was his fighting.*
> *When he would drink from a horn, / He would drink as much as four; / When into battle he came / He slew as would a hundred.*
> *Unless God should accomplish it, / Cei's death would be unattainable.*
> *Worthy Cei and Llachau / Used to fight battles, / Before the pain of livid spears [ended the conflict].*
> *On the top of Ystarfingun / Cei slew nine witches. / Worthy Cei went to Ynys Mon / To destroy lions. / Little protection did his shield offer / Against Palug's Cat.'*

The nine witches slain by Cei according to Arthur interestingly also feature later in our story.

After being tormented by Cei, Peredur sets out from the court of Arthur in a bid to regain his honour. In quick time, Peredur fights and defeats no less than sixteen knights in single combat. Later on his travels, Peredur meets separately two of his uncles. The role played by the uncles in the story of Peredur is taken by the characters of Gornemant of Gohort and the Fisher King in Chrétien's *Perceval* and Gurnemanz and Anfortas in Wolfram's *Parzival*.

The first uncle he meets instructs him in the use of arms and tells him not to question the significance of what he will later see. Peredur then ventures on and meets the second uncle. It is in the castle of his second uncle that the Grail is revealed to Peredur.

Here comes the crunch! Hold the front page! The Grail that is revealed to Peredur is not the cup of Christ but a purely pagan symbolic artefact, a man's severed head placed upon a salver! In the tale of *Peredur the Son of Evrawc* it is this man's head, surrounded by a profusion of blood, not the Holy Chalice, which is reunited with the bloody lance.

This part of the story clearly demonstrates the dichotomy present in British spirituality at this time, the prevalence of both Christian and pagan beliefs simultaneously pervading.

Peredur is portrayed in the story as being a Christian. Before setting out on his adventure, Peredur is told by his mother 'wherever thou seest a church, repeat there thy paternoster (Lord's Prayer) unto it'.

It has been suggested that Peredur was selected as the central character in the Grail story on account of him being a descendent of Jesus and, therefore, a continuation of Jesus's bloodline. A genealogy contained in the 'Laws of Hywel Dda' traces the ancestry of Coel Hen back to 'Aballach', supposedly the first-century ruler connected to the family of Jesus Christ. Peredur in turn, of course, can be traced back through his paternal line to Aballach. This connection predates medieval stories of Grail quests.

And yet, the Grail revealed to Peredur, a severed head, is straight out of the playbook of pagan symbolism. The ancient British were Celts, and in Celtic culture, the head was a deeply religious symbol. Sometimes, severed heads were used to represent deities. They were icons of supernatural wisdom and power as well as being a source of fertility, prosperity and healing. The Celts believed the human head housed the soul and was capable of independent life after the death of the body.

Perhaps the most famous example of Celtic head culture is Bran's head. Bran the Blessed was a giant Celtic deity who, according to Welsh mythology, was crowned king of the island (Britain). According to legend, when Bran was mortally wounded, he asked his companions to cut off his head. He told them to take his head with them on their wanderings, and it would provide them with marvellous entertainment. He said that his head would remain alive so long as they did not take it through a certain forbidden door. If they were to do so, they would find themselves back in the real world and would remember all their sorrows. The companions were to take Bran's head to the White Mount in London, the future site of the Tower of London, and bury it there. As long as it remained buried, it would safeguard Britain from invasion.

After seeing the severed head on the salver at his uncle's castle, Peredur continues on his journey, staying with the nine witches or sorceresses of Gloucester, who must be the same nine witches slain by Cei according to King Arthur's testament in 'Pa Gur yv y Porthaur'.

Peredur then returns to the court of Arthur and falls in love with Angharad Golden Hand, a beautiful maiden, providing romantic interest in the tale.

However, the love Peredur feels for Angharad seems to disappear as quickly as it came, and in an ancillary plot of the story, Peredur happens upon a beautiful lady, who it later transpires is the Empress of Constantinople. The lady warns Peredur that he will encounter a monster, known as the Addanc, and that the Addanc will slay him as it had slain many before. But the lady offers Peredur a way out

The mysterious severed head being shown to Peredur by the king in T.W Rolleston, *Myths and Legends of the Celtic Race*, George G. Harrap, 1912.

of his quandary. If he promises his love to her, she will give him a magical stone that will make him invisible to the monster. Peredur, with Angharad Golden Hand out of the picture, agrees to the deal, proclaiming it was love at first sight for him. Needless to say, Peredur encounters the Addanc and with the magic stone in his hand duly slays it by first thrusting his lace into it and then chopping off its head. After this, Peredur visits the empress who conveys her gratitude to him for slaying the monster and keeping his promise. In thanks for this, Peredur is entertained by the empress for a period of fourteen years. This is where one version of the story, contained in Peniarth MS 7, the earliest extant manuscript, concludes.

After further escapades, Peredur learns that the head revealed on the salver was that of his cousin, who was killed by the Sorceresses of Gloucester. Arthur and his knights then exact revenge on the nine witches of Gloucester slaying them all. And this is where the story ends.

In the latter part of the story, Peredur is referred to as 'Peredur of the long lance'. As we have discussed earlier, this is a nod to his obligation to avenge the Lord of the Fens for taking his father's lands from him.

Whilst the original Grail revealed to Peredur was a severed human head, over time, the Grail changes form, and by the time Peredur becomes Parzival, the Grail has become the Holy Grail, the cup used by Christ at the Last Supper and the cup used by Joseph of Arimathea to catch Jesus's blood at the crucifixion. The Grail first appears as the Holy Chalice or Cup in Robert de Boron's 'Grail Story Joseph d'Aramathie' written in the late-twelfth century.

It was Boron's work coupled with stories of Joseph of Arimathea that inspired the legend of the Holy Grail being buried in the ground below Glastonbury Tor.

According to this legend, Joseph first came to Britain as a merchant to buy Cornish tin. On one occasion, he brought with him the boy Jesus and built the first church on the site of Glastonbury Abbey, constructing it using wattle and daub. It is also alleged that after the crucifixion, Joseph became a missionary and returned to Britain carrying with him the Holy Grail. Joseph is said to have buried the Holy Grail in the ground below Glastonbury Tor and, as if by magic, a spring erupted on the site where he had buried it. Anyone who drank water from the spring was said to have been given the gift of eternal youth. The spring is now known as Chalice Well.

Boron's work upon which this legend is based is a pure work of fiction though, emanating from *Peredur the Son of Evrawc* in which as we have already discovered the Grail is a severed human head.

To see the Grail as a physical object rather than a symbolic object is a mistake. This was the mistake Rahn and the Nazis made. The symbolic meaning, or the truth of the Grail, the truth the Nazis never found, the truth that cost Rahn his life is what we shall now uncover.

Chapter 17

The Truth of the Grail

We have already established that over time the Grail story metamorphosed from being a pagan incarnation to Christian one. The story is not a straight retelling of the truth, but rather an allegorical tale set in the context of known history based on oral traditions. In addition, we have established the romances, *Peredur the Son of Evrawc*, *Perceval* and *Parzival* are all versions of the same allegorical tale.

An allegory, by definition, is an expression using symbolic fictional figures and/or actions of truths or generalizations about human existence. Allegories can take the form of stories, plays, poems or pictures and often relate to morals, religion or politics.

Allegories were used as far back as the time of the Roman Empire when myths were not only sacred texts about the gods but stories that needed to be interpreted to unveil hidden symbolism.

Similarly, Christianity used allegoric stories to convey teachings with a deeper meaning. Some stories in the Old Testament can be seen as allegories of New Testament events. For example, the story of Jonah and the Whale, with Jonah being first swallowed then spit out alive by the whale three days later, can be interpreted as Jesus's death and resurrection, three days after his body was placed in the tomb.

The use of allegory was not a Christian invention though, it was present in oral traditions throughout the ancient world, and the story of *Peredur the Son of Evrawc* is one such example.

In an oral tradition, such as those that found their way into *The Mabinogion*, by definition very little was written down, and what was written was only available to a very few. Medieval audiences would have interpreted the tales from within the context of their own lives and lore. Over the years, decades and centuries, oral traditions would have grown and developed with additional events and details bolted on to spice up the story for a particular gathering. The interpretation of allegory would have been open to the imagination of the storytellers and the listeners, who between them would tease out the meaning of the themes contained within the tale.

Our task now is to tease out the meaning of the themes contained within the Grail story and thus uncover the truth of the Grail!

In an interesting twist, we will make significant use of Walter Johannes Stein, possibly Hitler's first choice Grail hunter, who defected to Britain in 1933.

Although Walter Johannes Stein, the Austrian Grail researcher, did not delve into the Peredur version of the Grail story, he certainly

Walter Johannes Stein, c.1930.

twigged on to the Parzival version being allegorical and extensively explored the symbolism contained within it.

Stein left for Britain in 1933, having regularly lectured in Stuttgart, before Himmler could recruit him to search for the Grail on behalf of the Nazis. Stein was part Jewish on his mother's side, and this may well have figured significantly in him making the decision to leave Germany the year the Nazis came to power. That year, 1933, was also the year Rahn's first work, *Crusade against the Grail*, was published and the year Rahn was recruited into the SS by Himmler.

Stein's thoughts on the Grail story have been captured in *The Death of Merlin*, a collection of essays that were first published, or delivered as lectures, by Stein in the 1920s and 1930s. In one of these essays, focussing on Wolfram's version of the tale, he explores the purpose of the central character, Parzival: 'But now the Grail Story goes on and describes just how such a man actually finds his way to the Holy Grail. Precisely this kind of soul is able to find its way to the highest spiritual possession.'[1]

Stein clearly understood that the Grail story was a metaphor for the journey towards spiritual enlightenment or spiritual possession. Furthermore, Stein makes specific reference to the British people and their relevance to the Grail story:

> *'The English-speaking people have developed a new consciousness for themselves, and this consciousness is to be found exemplified in the figure of Parzival. This too is a discovery of Rudolf Steiner. He calls the peculiar nature of the consciousness of the English-speaking peoples, and in particular of the British themselves. The "Consciousness soul". And he describes Parzival as being the typical representative of this consciousness soul.'*[2]

Stein had been a student of Rudolf Steiner, a social scientist with a keen interest in spirituality, who had formed the Anthroposophical Society, a spiritual movement in Germany. Rudolf Steiner was hugely influential in Stein's thinking. This last passage strongly points towards Stein being aware of the British roots of the Grail saga and its relevance to the British people, with references to 'English-speaking peoples' and the 'British themselves'. This view would clearly have put him very much at odds with the view taken by Hitler and Himmler, who were trying to create an Aryan Germanic ownership of the Grail story. Furthermore, Stein was in no doubt that the Grail story was allegorical, and the Grail itself was a metaphor for spiritual enlightenment. This was not what the Nazis wanted to hear; they wanted to find a physical object, the actual Holy Chalice. No wonder Stein skedaddled to Britain in 1933, when the Nazis came to power in Germany.

It is also likely that, in his heart of hearts, Rahn knew this truth about the Grail before he died, but by then, it was too late. He had promised the Nazis he would find the Holy Chalice and in doing so had dug himself a hole he couldn't climb out of.

In teasing out the meaning of the allegory, it is *Peredur the Son of Evrawc*, the original version of the Grail story, that we will primarily focus on. The first Grail hero, Peredur, as we have already established, was a Dark Age warrior. He emanated from a time when the British 'consciousness soul', referenced by Stein, was in a state of flux. York, the ancestral home of Peredur, had been proclaimed a bishopric in AD 314 under the rule of Constantine the Great, who was made emperor in the city. But many Britons still, at least in part, clung to a belief in the ancient British gods. This duality of belief is evidenced by Romano-British artefacts held in the British Museum decorated with both pagan and Christian symbols.

The introduction of the Empress of Constantinople into the story of *Peredur the Son of Evrawc* is interesting. The ancillary plot involving her is key to unravelling the allegory. The Empress of Constantinople is Helena of Constantinople, the mother of Constantine the Great, who was crowned in York and founded the city bearing his name, Constantinople, in AD 324, making it the capital of the Roman Empire.

The young Constantine had been taken away from his mother, Helena, as a child and held hostage by Roman officials seeking to put pressure on his father. One night, Constantine escaped his captors and found his father, a soldier, in Gaul. Together, they sailed to Britain to fight the Scots mounting raids over Hadrian's Wall. Constantine fared well in the army, enjoying success in battle and rising through the ranks. His success culminated in him being declared emperor by his troops in York on the 25 July 306. One of his first acts as emperor was to bring his mother Helena to court, elevating her position and giving her the title *Noblissima Femina* thus ending their fourteen-year separation. Which, perhaps not entirely coincidentally, exactly matches the fourteen-year period Peredur is entertained by Helena in the story after he has killed the Addanc. More on this later.

Helena was known for her benevolent nature and her sympathetic attitude towards Christians. After her son, Constantine, granted protection to Christians in AD 313, she was baptised at the age of 63 and became an important figure in the Christian church, building many churches. Helena was beatified after her death and is known as Helena of Constantinople to distinguish her from other St Helenas or Helens.

Both the memory of Constantine, his mother Helena and the Christian faith they championed remained present in York long after the demise of the Roman Empire. That Christianity pervaded York in the Dark Ages is indicated by an abundance of pilgrimage flasks dating from the fifth century found in the city and now housed in the Yorkshire Museum.

Constantine's significance to the Christian church and his association with the city of York were remembered in AD 627 when King Edwin of Northumbria, newly converted from paganism to Christianity, built the first church dedicated to St Peter on the ruins of the Roman principia in York, the site of Constantine's proclamation as emperor. This seventh-century church was the forerunner of the present-day minster. Edwin's conversion to Christianity is also commemorated by the Lilla Cross (see Appendix IV).

Although it disappeared a long time ago, there was once a church dedicated to Constantine's mother, St Helen, which stood on Aldwark, one of the oldest streets in York, where, according to legend, Constantine was buried.

In a distortion of the truth, it passed into British mythology that Constantine was born in Britain to a British mother Helen. According to legend, Helen, the mother of Constantine, was the daughter of Coel Hen from whom Peredur was descended. This is untrue, but it shows how significant Constantine and Helena were as figures in British history.

In the Grail story, Helena of Constantinople is representative of the Christian faith. Her position of eminence within the Christian church would have been well known to the post-Roman British and her representing the church would be an easy jump for them to make. Peredur's chance meeting with Helena of Constantinople, and his making a deal with her is symbolic of him making a pact with the church. In promising his love to her, he has faith that the magical stone she gives him will protect him from the danger he faces in encountering the Addanc. The Addanc is a monster who has killed many innocents and is representative of evil in the world.

The magical stone Helena gives Peredur to hold in his hand when he goes forth into the Addanc's lair is symbolic of Peredur putting his faith in God and the church, and carrying his faith with him in facing a challenge. Similarities can be drawn here with the stone mentioned in the Book of Revelation in the Bible: 'He that hath an ear, let him hear what the Spirit saith unto the churches; To him that overcometh will I give to eat of the hidden manna, and will give him a white stone, and in the stone a new name written, which no man knoweth saving he that receiveth it' (Revelation 2:17, KJV).

Having struck the deal with Helena, Peredur sets out in search of the Addanc:

> *'He continued along to a river valley, and the edges of the valley were wooded and on each side of the river there were flat meadows. On one side of the river, he could see a flock of white sheep, and on the other he could see a flock of black: when one of the white sheep bleated, one of the black sheep would come across and turn white, and when one of the black sheep bleated, one of the white sheep would come across and turn black.'*[3]

This passage from the Grail story sets out the state of the nation's 'consciousness soul' at the time, as termed by Walter Johannes Stein. The sheep are representative of people switching between traditional pagan beliefs and Christian beliefs. This scenario fits exactly with the state of religious flux occurring in Britain at the time, as we have already identified. The passage continues: 'He could see a tall tree on the riverbank, and one half of it was burning from its roots to its tip, but the other half had fresh leaves on it.' This further emphasises the point. It is a direct take on the story of the 'burning bush' contained within the Bible. Incidentally, this story is common to Christianity, Islam and Judaism. In Exodus 3:1–4, in the Bible, it says that Moses was tending to his flock of sheep:

> *'And the angel of the Lord appeared unto him in a flame of fire out of the midst of a bush; and he looked, and behold, the bush burned with fire, and the bush was not consumed. And Moses said, I will now turn aside, and see this great sight, why the bush is not burnt. And when the Lord saw that he turned aside to see, God called unto him out of the midst of the bush, and said, Moses, Moses. And he said, Here am I.'*

It is blindingly obvious what the allegory is representing here. One half of the sheep got the same message from God that Moses did, the other half simply did not.

As we know, whilst the nation was in a fifty–fifty state regarding their belief in a monotheistic God, Peredur, our hero, had already made his covenant with God, represented by the deal he made with Helena.

Having passed through the valley of sheep, Peredur reaches a fork in the road. He listens to advice about where each path will take him and chooses to follow the path that will lead him to the challenge of fighting the Addanc. Peredur follows the path to the cave where the Addanc lives and enters the cave with the stone, representing his faith in the Lord, in one hand and his lance in the other. Armed with his faith and the lance, Peredur slays the Addanc and so triumphs over evil.

When Peredur next meets the Empress Helena, she says to him: 'Goodly Peredur, remember the faith thou didst pledge me when I gave thee the stone, and thou didst kill the Addanc.'

In saying this, Helena is reminding Peredur that it was his faith in God that enabled him to overcome evil. Peredur is duly rewarded by being entertained by Helena for a period of fourteen years. This could be interpreted as him receiving a celestial reward akin to heaven.

The pagan myth of Chimaera was often similarly used as an allegory for Christ's triumph over evil in Roman times (see Appendix II). This is where Peniarth MS 7 ends.

In other manuscripts, the story continues in a jumbled manner, with Peredur learning of the 'Castle of Wonders'. He then embarks on a search for the castle, which leads to him being imprisoned and fighting in tournaments along the way. He is then given directions to the 'Castle of Wonder' by the daughter of his former captor.

Peredur follows the directions to the castle and enters. Whereupon, he sees a magical chess game taking place with the pieces moving themselves. After the side Peredur was supporting are defeated and their opponents exclaimed their joy at victory, Peredur could not hold back his anger and launched the chessboard into the lake by the castle.

A black maiden then enters the room and chastises Peredur for throwing the chessboard. The black maiden then explains to Peredur the error of his ways, telling him that he has lost the chessboard belonging to the empress (Helena of Constantinople), which was dearer to her than all her kingdom. She then offers him a way out, telling him that to recover the chessboard he must go to the Castle of Ysbidinongyl, where he will find a black man who lays waste to the dominions of the empress. If Peredur can slay the black man, he will recover the chessboard. But then comes a warning that if he goes there, he will not come back alive.

Undaunted, Peredur proceeds to the Castle of Ysbidinongyl and finds the black man, who he defeats in combat. The black man pleads for mercy, which Peredur grants on condition that the chessboard is restored to its place. Then the maiden reappears and berates Peredur for not carrying through with killing his adversary who lays waste to all the possessions of the empress. She tells him that the chessboard is not back in place and that he must go through with the killing. Peredur duly goes back and slays the man.

Peredur returns to the Castle of Wonders and enquires of the maiden the whereabouts of the empress. To which she replies he will not see

Alfred Fredericks, *Peredur and the Chessmen* from Lanier, Sidney, *Knightly Legends of Wales*, Charles Scribner's Sons, 1881.

the empress until he has slain the monster that dwells in yonder forest. She then sets Peredur the task of killing the fearsome stag-like monster and offers him a small dog belonging to the empress to lure the stag towards him. Peredur executes the plan and slays the stag, cutting off its head with his sword.

No sooner has he done this then a lady appears riding a horse. The lady admonishes Peredur for killing her stag and tells him that he can make amends by going to a grove where a stone tomb stands, there he must challenge a man to fight three times.

When Peredur arrives at the grove and challenges any man to fight him three times, a black man on horseback comes out from under the stone tomb. The men fight, and every time Peredur knocks the black man from his horse, the black man remounts. Peredur then dismounts and draws his sword, but as he does, his opponent disappears with both their horses. Having lost sight of his opponent, Peredur carries on along the way until he reaches the 'Castle of Wonders'.

He enters and is greeted by Gwalchmai, his old compadre. It is then that Peredur is approached by a yellow-haired youth who has shape-shifted throughout the second part of this story, taking on amongst other forms that of the maiden who first told Peredur about the 'Castle of Wonders'. The youth tells Peredur that it was he who paraded the bloody head on the salver in front of him at the castle of his uncle and that the head was that of his cousin, who had been killed by the sorceresses of Gloucester. The same sorceresses had attacked his uncle and left him lame. The youth then predicts that Peredur will avenge these things. With that, Peredur and Gwalchmai send word to the court of Arthur for reinforcements to be sent. When Arthur arrives with reinforcements, they band together and set about attacking the sorceresses until none are left. And this is how the story of the 'Castle of Wonders' ends.

This second part of thc talc is clcarly a story of vengeance of the Old Testament 'an eye for an eye' kind. It could be that this continuation was added as a rallying call for the crusades and the recapture of Jerusalem.

The Eastern, or Byzantine, Empire, with its capital in Constantinople, had held sway over Jerusalem until they surrendered the city to Caliph Umar and the Muslim forces outside the gates, after a bloodless siege had taken place.

Under a pact known as the Umariyya Covenant, guarantees of civil and religious liberty to Christians were given in exchange for the payment of a taxation levied upon them. This guarantee also applied to Jews, who had not been allowed to inhabit the city under Byzantine rule. By the eleventh century though, things had become more unsettled, and this led to uneasiness and suffering among the Christian population in Jerusalem.

It may be that the 'Castle of Wonders' represented Jerusalem with Peredur, Arthur, Gwalchmai et al being the crusaders, and in an outdated tale of its time, it was written by a medieval evangelical Christian author, the Sorceresses of Gloucester, who represented the Islamic rulers of Jerusalem.

This would make sense in the context that it is inferred the 'Castle of Wonders' is the property of the Empress Helena of Constantinople. Helena had strong connections with Jerusalem. Eusebius, the Greek historian of Christianity who lived in the fourth century, tells us that Helena had destroyed a temple erected in honour of the roman god Venus on the supposed site of Jesus's tomb. According to legend, under the supervision of Helena, the ground in Jerusalem was excavated and three crosses were found. In a test to determine the true cross, Helena had a sick woman brought to the crosses and had the woman touch each cross in turn. When the woman touched the third cross, she was healed, and this cross was declared the True Cross by Helena. It is also claimed that Helena found the nails of the cross and the Holy Tunic in Jerusalem. Constantine had the Church of the Holy Sepulchre built on the site of Helena's discovery.

When the maiden remonstrates with Peredur for not slaying the man who 'lays waste all the possessions of the Empress', these possessions could be any number of religious artefacts associated with Helena and Jerusalem.

This all points to the second part of the story of *Peredur the Son of Evrawc* being an allegory for the First Crusade, which took place in 1096.

However, if we accept the premise of the story being an allegory about the crusades and re-examine the story more closely, other things begin to fall in place.

Firstly, the stone tomb where Peredur is to go and call out for a fight, given what we now know, is surely the site of Jesus's burial in Jerusalem. This leads immediately to the significance of him being instructed to fight three times. This must relate to three crusades!

The actual term used by Lady Charlotte Guest in her translation of *Peredur the Son of Evrawc* is a *cromlech*. Ring any bells? No? So, to the dictionary, where *cromlech* is defined (in Wales) as a megalithic tomb consisting of a large flat stone laid on upright ones (a dolmen) or (in Brittany) as a circle of standing stones. The Welsh definition is most appropriate and seems to fit what we might expect the tomb of Christ to look like. All is well!

It fits that, in the story, the instruction for Peredur to fight three times comes from the maiden who is a representative of St Helena, this effectively makes the instruction a command from God!

Now the imprisonment of Peredur in a castle while searching for the 'Castle of Wonders' has significance as well. This must be representative of Richard I, otherwise known as Richard the Lionheart, a key figure in the crusades, being imprisoned in Duke Leopold's castle at Dürnstein on the Danube in 1192. Let's examine the imprisonment of Peredur more closely and see how this theory stands up under the microscope.

Starting with the location of Peredur's imprisonment, we have the following text 'Go over yonder mountain, and on the other side of the mountain thou wilt come to a river, and in the valley wherein the river runs is a King's palace.' Dürnstein Castle stands on the bank of the River Danube in the Alpine Wachau valley. Perfect fit!

Peredur's captor was a king, Tick! Duke Leopold was in fact Leopold V Duke of Austria – effectively a king!

The circumstances surrounding Peredur's capture and release are also worth a look here. On approaching the castle, Peredur is greeting by a high-ranking man (the king of the castle) out hunting with his men. The man invites Peredur to go to his castle, where his daughter will look after him. When Peredur arrives at the castle, he is warmly welcomed by the noble's daughter and a good deal of flirting between the two takes place. The page who escorted Peredur to the castle sees this and runs back to tell the king. The king instructs the page to gather some strong men and to seize Peredur and imprison him. The king's daughter pleads with the king to have Peredur released but the king refuses. The king's daughter continues to communicate with Peredur, and when Peredur hears a tumult of shouting occurring outside of the castle, he asks the king's daughter what is happening. The king's daughter tells Peredur that a rival earl and his forces have come to town and combat is about to take place. Peredur promises to go back to his prison if he is allowed to take part in the combat. The king's daughter provides Peredur with arms and armour as well as a horse and a red tunic to wear over his armour. Peredur joins the combat, slaying all-comers then returns to his prison before nightfall. This pattern repeats for three days and three nights, and then on the fourth day, Peredur kills the rival earl. In thanks, the king offers his daughter's hand in marriage to Peredur, but Peredur politely declines the offer telling the king he 'came not here to woo' but to 'seek tidings of the Castle of Wonders!'[4]

So how does this little episode tie in with Richard I being imprisoned in a castle in Austria? Well, sadly it doesn't. The nearest we get to this is the romance of Blondel. Which unfortunately is a romance of the story variety not the traditional kind. According to legend, Blondel was a troubadour who was travelling from castle to castle singing King Richard's favourite song in order to find him. Finally, when he was performing his song in Dürnstein, the king answered by singing the second verse. Thereupon, Blondel arranged for King Richard to be freed. However, it still seems likely that Peredur's imprisonment is a nod to the imprisonment of Richard I.

To tie things up here, we need to check dates and see how these tie in. If the command to fight three times is linked to three crusades, the Third Crusade to Jerusalem took place between 1189 and 1192 and was led by Richard I of England and Philip II of Spain. During the Third Crusade, King Richard twice led the crusaders to Jerusalem, yet on both occasions was forced to retreat after coming within sight of the holy city. This accounts for the 'as often as Peredur cast the black man to the earth, he would jump up again'. This could also refer to the Muslim forces fighting back after the first two crusades, which took place in quick succession. The second part of *Peredur the Son of Evrawc*, must be an allegory for the Third Crusade to Jerusalem, with Peredur cast as the crusading Richard the Lionheart.

Conclusion

We can now begin to date the writing of *Peredur the Son of Evrawc* a little more accurately.

It definitely seems the story was written in two parts; the first part being an allegory for the conversion of the British to Christianity from their pagan beliefs in Celtic gods; the second part being an allegory for the Third Crusade.

Everything in the first part is consistent with the Dark Ages. The names of the characters can all be traced and are contemporary with the period the story is set in. The premise of the allegory is also consistent with this (approximately fifth to eighth centuries). Geographically, the story holds up and Helena, Constantine's mother, and her association with the Christian church would have been known about in York, where Peredur came from. The setting is largely contemporary with this period as we have established earlier. Peredur makes a logical choice for the hero, having been a key protagonist at the Battle of Ardderyd, which was a confrontation fought between fellow Britons with differing religious views; some accepting Christianity others clinging to their pagan beliefs. Peredur was likely in real life a champion of Christianity just as he is portrayed in the story. There is every reason to believe that the first part of the story is the writing up of a Dark Age allegorical myth.

The key thing to consider here is if the story of *Peredur the Son of Evrawc* came into being in the high Middle Ages, why would the object serving as the Grail be a decapitated human head? This must have been a story based upon an earlier myth when the British still at least in part held pagan beliefs. There is nothing about this first part of the story that refers to anything that would not have been known about in the Dark Ages. As with all oral stories, new elements to the story will have been added to it over the years and retellings, but the story is firmly rooted to Britain in the fifth to eighth centuries.

The second part of the story was clearly added on at a later date. There is a clear ending to the first part – 'And Peredur was entertained by the Empress by fourteen years, as the story relates.' This is where Peniarth MS 7 ends. So, the original Grail was a severed human head!

The second part of the story was contrived significantly later than the first. We know this because the allegory relates to the Third Crusade in which Richard the Lionheart, one of the most famous English king of all time, took a lead role. It is an English tale, in contrast to the first part of *Peredur the Son of Evrawc*, which is a British or Celtic tale. The Third Crusade took place from 1189 to 1192. King Richard's imprisonment lasted from 1192 to 1194. So, the earliest the second part of the Peredur story could have been written is 1194.

Chrétien de Troyes wrote *Perceval* or *The Story of the Grail* for his patron Philip the Count of Flanders sometime between 1178 and 1191, when the count died. In the prologue, Chrétien claims to be working from a 'Story of the Grail' given to him by the count. At one point in Chrétien's tale, when Gawain is sent to find the bleeding lance, it is revealed as the lance that is destined to destroy the realm of Logres (England). This is a direct reference to a British response to the English or Saxons having taken control of a large part, if not all, of what is now England. The implication is that the revealment puts the story in the context of the British still having hope of the Saxons being defeated and vanquished. This 'hope' relates to a time in the Dark Ages, with a date between 450 and 650. The 'Story of the Grail' Chrétien was working from must have been part one of *Peredur the Son of Evrawc* contained in Peniarth MS 7.

Part two of *Peredur the Son of Evrawc* was written after Chrétien's *Perceval* and borrows from it the hero Perceval or Peredur learning of a family connection to the Grail. In Perceval's case, he is told by his hermit uncle that he (Perceval) is a close relative of the Fisher King and that the man being served with the Grail in the inner room is the Fisher King's father. Peredur is told by the yellow haired youth that the bloody head in the salver was that of his cousin.

Specific information that can be used to date the writing of *Parzival* is scarce, but it is reckoned Wolfram von Eschenbach, its author, must have been born around 1170 and have begun writing *Parzival* around 1197 or 1198. Without doubt later than both *Perceval* and part one of Peredur.

The term Grail emerged from the 'graal' (platter) owned by the Fisher King in Chrétien's *Perceval* or *The Story of the Grail*. In Chrétien's *Story of the Grail* the 'graal' or Grail is a bounteous platter upon which food miraculously appeared. This borrows from part one of Peredur being a take on the bloody head on the salver (see Appendix I – P Comparison).

The concept of the Grail being the Holy Chalice was introduced later by Robert de Boron. In his poem 'Joseph d'Aramathie', de Boron assimilates the Grail meal into the Last Supper, with Pontius Pilate giving the cup used at the Last Supper to Joseph of Arimathea, who uses it to catch Christ's blood at the crucifixion. In de Boron's poem, the Grail provides sustenance for Joseph when he is imprisoned in gaol. When fish are caught by Joseph's brother-in-law, Bron, for a sacred feast, the Grail is first referred to as the Holy Grail. The Holy Grail brings joy but is also able to distinguish true followers from false ones. Bron becomes the Rich Fisher and journeys to Britain with the Grail where Perceval awaits. The story then follows a similar pattern to Chrétien's *Perceval* with Bron taking the part of the Fisher King. Bron is a shortened form of Hebron, but it could also be that this is a nod to the Celtic legend of 'Bran's head'.

The true Grail story is the stem common to Peredur, Perceval and Parzival. Each element of the story of Peredur is evident in that of Perceval and Parzival up to and including the point where the severed head is revealed. The stories diverge dramatically after this point. This true Grail story is a British tale with British characters, British places and a son of York, Peredur, the hero.

The true Grail story is rooted in Celtic myth, with the bloody head on a salver, the Grail. This begs the question whose head was it? But that is a question for another time and perhaps even another book!

Appendix I

P Comparison

The table below shows elements common to each of the three versions of the Grail story we have discussed.

Peredur	**Perceval**	**Parzival**
Evrawc, Earl of the North, dies in combat along with six of his sons leaving the youngest, Peredur, to be raised by his mother. His mother takes counsel and decides it prudent to leave town for the wilderness of the woods. Peredur is thereby raised in isolation by his mother in the forest.	The knight Gahmuret comes home after being wounded and losing his wealth in combat. When Perceval's two brothers become knights and die in combat, Gahmuret dies of grief, leaving Perceval to be raised alone by his mother as a Welshman in the forest and in ignorance of his chivalry.	Gahmuret, having sought his fortune in the east, returns to Europe and fights in a tournament at Kanvoleis in Waleis. As the winner, he takes up his entitlement to marry Herzeloyde. Hearing that Baruc is besieged, he returns to the east, where he is killed, leaving Herzeloyde pregnant. Shortly after learning of his death, she bears Parzival and withdraws from courtly society to raise Parzival in the woods, where he is kept ignorant of his knighthood.
As he comes of age, Peredur meets a group of three knights, Gwalchmai, who was the son of Gwyar, Geneir Gwystyl and Owain, who was the son of Urien. Peredur leaves his mother and goes with them to the court of King Arthur.	After a chance meeting with five unnamed knights, Perceval leaves his mother to become a knight at the court of King Arthur.	When he encounters three knights while hunting in the forest, Parzival is overcome with desire to become a knight himself and takes up an invitation offered by the knights to ride with them to the court of King Arthur and be made a knight.

Peredur	Perceval	Parzival
Peredur comes across a tent inside of which is sitting a maiden. Remembering his mother's advice, Peredur treats the maiden courteously and accepts her offer of food and takes a jewel with the maiden's blessing. When the maiden's lord returns, she speaks highly of Peredur, extolling his virtues.	In an encounter with an unnamed maiden in a tent, Perceval forces kisses from her, forcibly takes her ring and helps himself to all the food and drink he can manage. When the maiden's sweetheart returns, he refuses to believe that Peredur forced himself upon the maiden despite her protestations and punishes her.	Parzival soon encounters Jeschute lying in a tent. Remembering his mother's advice to 'win a lady's ring and greeting' whenever he can, Parzival grapples with her and takes a ring from her, thus disgracing her in the eyes of her husband, Orlius, who thinks she has been unfaithful, and punishes her severely.
At the court of King Arthur, Peredur is ridiculed by the brutish Kay. Peredur takes up a challenge set by Kay, which he duly accomplishes, to take the horse and arms along with a goblet from a knight who had insulted Gwenhwyvar (Guinevere).	Perceval arrives at the court of King Arthur and is mocked by Kay. Peredur asks to be granted the Red Knight's armour, and Kay challenges him to dispossess the Red Knight of his armour. Peredur defeats and kills the Red Knight by thrusting a javelin through his eye. Perceval takes the dead knight's armour and horse.	After the Red Knight, Ither, has visited the court with unacceptable demands. Parzival begs to be given the Red Knight's armour, and Kay, whose role at court is often to mock and scorn, persuades Arthur to make this gift. It is a trick, of course, to provoke a fight between the foolish-looking boy and the Red Knight, but Parzival kills Ither with his hunting spear and takes the red armour for himself.
On his travels, Peredur meets two of his uncles. The first shows him how to bear arms and instructs him not to question the significance of what he sees.	Perceval rides away and comes to a castle by a river and the sea. He encounters a gentleman in ermine, Gornemant of Gohort, and they converse. Perceval asks for lodging, and Gornemant, or Gurnemanz according to Wolfram, begins to teach him how to conduct himself as a knight. Perceval expresses	Parzival rides on and soon meets the old knight Gurnemanz, who trains him to become a perfect knight.

Peredur	Perceval	Parzival
	concern about his mother, whom he saw faint as he was leaving her. The next morning, Gornemant gives him clothing and a sword, conferring on him knighthood. Gornemant advises Perceval to not be too talkative or prone to gossip, to find a maiden or woman whom he can console, to go to church and not to claim publicly that he was taught by his mother. Perceval departs to find his mother.	
Peredur enters the castle of the second uncle and is presented with a magical sword. Then, a mighty spear with three streams of blood flowing from the point to the ground and a man's head on a salver are brought before him.	Perceval enters the castle of the Fisher King. During dinner with the Fisher King, Perceval is bestowed with the gift of a sword with special properties before several objects are paraded before Perceval – a bleeding white lance, candelabra and the Grail, a serving dish made of finest gold and decorated with gems.	At a lake, Parzival encounters the Angler, Anfortas, who urges him to seek lodging for the night at a nearby castle – Munsalvaesche. Parzival enters the castle, where at a banquet, he witnesses the marvellous rituals of the Grail and the Bloody Lance. The Grail is carried by Anfortas the Angler, who turns out to be the lord of this castle and presents Parzival with a sword whose blade is the source of great wonders.

Appendix II

Chimaera

The Roman villa at Lullingstone in Kent provides significant evidence of Romano-British Christianity. Built perhaps as early as the AD 80s, Lullingstone Villa reached the peak of luxury in the mid-fourth century when its spectacular mosaics were laid. As well as having a 'house church', the main mosaic panel in the audience chamber tells the story of Bellerophon, mounted on the winged-horse Pegasus, slaying the Chimaera, a fire-breathing lion monster beneath him. The pagan myth depicted in this scene was often used as an allegory for Christ's triumph over evil in Roman times.

Mosaic from Lullingstone Villa telling the story of Bellerophon slaying the Chimaera.

Appendix III

Barnburgh – A Case Study

Nowhere is the interweaving of Christian and pagan Celtic tradition more demonstrably illustrated than in the site of St Helen's Chapel near Barnburgh. A beacon of Christianity set in land littered with references to Celtic mythology. The chapel, which measured approximately 14m by 7m, is no longer standing. What remains is enclosed in a small copse set just off St Helen's Lane.

The ruins lie close to what was part of the Roman Ricknield Street now Hangman Stone Road. It is believed that the chapel was dedicated to Ellen, the Celtic goddess of armies and roads but was later rededicated by the early Christians to St Helen, the mother of Emperor Constantine.

Close to the site is St Helen's Spring, which was at one time reputed to have valuable medicinal properties. The Celts observed the practice of regarding water and in particular wells (believed to give access to the underworld) as having sacred qualities. With the conversion to Christianity, the pagan deities to whom the wells were dedicated were 'converted' to Holy Wells and replaced by a Christian saint – St Helen and Our Lady being popular names.

Also, nearby to St Helen's Chapel is the River Don, the fields of Maisbeli and Ludwell hill. Maisbeli is ancient British for the field of Beli. All these geographical features take their name from Celtic deities. In Middle Welsh literature and genealogies, Beli Mawr or 'Beli the Great' was the father of Llud Llaw Ereint (Llud of the Silver Hand) and the husband of Don.

Barnburgh, St Helen's Chapel and Ludwell Hill all fall within the boundaries of the ancient British kingdom of Elmet, whose southern boundary was the River Don. Indeed, High Melton, approximately 1.5 miles east of Barnburgh, was once known as High Melton-in-Elmet. This is the very landscape in which the story of *Peredur the Son of Evrawc* was set.

Appendix IV

Lilla Cross

The oldest Christian relic in Yorkshire is Lilla Cross, situated on Fylingdales Moor. The present cross is believed to date from the tenth century. However, the original cross was placed on the same site in the seventh century by King Edwin and would have been contemporary with the time the oral traditions of Peredur became prevalent in Britain.

Lilla Cross, Yorkshire's oldest Christian relic, stands on Fylingdales Moor. Dating back to the 10th century, it marks the site of an original 7th-century cross erected by King Edwin.

Notes

Part I: The Nazi Quest for the Holy Grail

1. Rahn, Otto (1937), *The Court of Lucifer: A Voyage with Europe's Benevolent Ghosts* (translated by Christopher Jones), Inner Traditions, p.156

Prologue

1. Kirkpatrick, Sidney (2011), *Hitler's Holy Relics*, Simon & Schuster

Chapter 1: The Early Life of Otto Tahn

1. *The Court of Lucifer: A Voyage with Europe's Benevolent Ghosts*, p.109

Chapter 2: Rahn's Quest for the Holy Grail Commences

1. Rahn, Otto (2006), *Crusade Against the Grail*, Inner Traditions International, p.96

Chapter 3: Hitler, Wagner and *Parsifal*

1. Hitler, Adolf (2023), *Mein Kampf*, Jaico Publishing House, pp.27–28
2. Hall, David Ian (2017), 'Wagner, Hitler, and Germany's Rebirth after the First War', *War in History*, Vol. 24, No. 2 (April), Sage, pp.154–75
3. Rauschning, Hermann (1939), *Hitler Speaks*, Eyre & Spottiswoode, p. 227
4. *The Daily Telegraph*, 25 April 1935

Chapter 4: Ludwig II

1. 'King Ludwig II of Bavaria', Neuschwanstein Castle website (www.neuschwanstein.de/englisch/ludwig/biography.htm), accessed 4 March 2023
2. *Mein Kampf*, pp.239–240

Chapter 6: Wewelsburg Castle

1. Padfield, Peter (2013), *Himmler Reichsführer-SS*, Thistle Publishing, p.132
2. Crossland, David, 'New Exhibition Explodes Myth of SS Castle Wewelsburg', Speigel International website (www.spiegel.de), accessed 4 March 2023

Chapter 7: Religious Implications of the Grail Hunt

1. Steigmann-Gall, Richard (2004), *The Holy Reich, Nazi Concepts of Christianity, 1919–1945*, Cambridge University Press, p.14
2. Rosenberg, Alfred (1949), *Memoirs of Alfred Rosenberg*, Ziff-Davis Publishing, p.88.
3. *Memoirs of Alfred Rosenberg*, p.95
4. Stein, Leo (1941), 'Niemoller Speaks! An Exclusive Report by One Who Lived in Prison with the Famous German Pastor Who Defied Adolf Hitler', *The National Jewish Monthly*, May, pp.284–5, pp.301–2

Chapter 8: Rahn's Theory and the Cathars

1. Rahn, Otto (2006), *Crusade Against the Grail*, Inner Traditions, p.35
2. *Crusade Against the Grail*, p.39, p.40
3. *Crusade Against the Grail*, p.39
4. O'Shea, Stephen (2001), *The Perfect Heresy, The Revolutionary Life and Death of the Medieval Cathars*, Profile Books, p.101
5. *Crusade Against the Grail*, pp.176–7

Chapter 9: Christian Relic?

1. *Crusade Against the Grail*, p.115
2. Tennyson, Alfred (1870), *The Holy Grail and Other Poems*, J.E. Tilton and Company, p.18
3. Prelude to Act 1 of *Parsifal* (www.monsalvat.no/prelact1.htm), accessed 18 March 2023
4. Wagner, Cosima (1978), *Cosima Wagner's Diaries Volume I 1869–1877*, Harcourt Brace Jovanovich, p.984

Chapter 10: Rahn's Search for the Grail Continues

1. *The Court of Lucifer: A Voyage with Europe's Benevolent Ghosts* (1937), p.29
2. *Crusade Against the Grail*, p.78
3. *The Court of Lucifer: A Voyage with Europe's Benevolent Ghosts*, p.50
4. *The Court of Lucifer: A Voyage with Europe's Benevolent Ghosts*, p.163
5. *The Court of Lucifer: A Voyage with Europe's Benevolent Ghosts*, p.187
6. *Crusade Against the Grail*, p.99, p.101

Chapter 11: The Holy Lance

1. Roland, Paul (2018), *The Nazis and the Occult*, Arcturus Publishing, p.40

Chapter 12: The End of Rahn

1. Graddon, Nigel (2008), *Otto Rahn and the Quest for the Holy Grail*, Adventures Unlimited Press, p.141

Part II: Peredur – The Truth of the Grail

1. Loomis, Roger Sherman (1991), 'The Origins and Growth of Arthurian Romance' in *The Grail: From Celtic Myth to Christian Symbol*, Princeton University Press, pp.7–19

Chapter 15: The Historical Peredur

1. Morris, John (2001), *The Age of Arthur: A History of the British Isles from 350 to 650*, Phoenix Press, p.54
2. Williams, Robert (1987), *Facsimile Reproduction of Y Seint Greal, The Holy Grail*, edited and translated in 1876, Jones
3. Bromwich, Rachael (2014), *Trioedd Ynys Prydein: The Triads of the Island of Britain*, University of Wales Press, p.11
4. Skene, William F. (1868), *The Four Ancient Books of Wales*, Edmonston and Douglas, p.328
5. *The Four Ancient Books of Wales*, p.328
6. Tolstoy, Nikolai (1985), *The Quest for Merlin*, Little, Brown and Company, p.49
7. Collingwood, R. G. and Myres, John Nowell Linton (1937), *Roman Britain and English Settlements*, Oxford History of England, OUP

8. Bromwich, Rachael (2014), *Trioedd Ynys Prydein: The Triads of the Island of Britain*, University of Wales Press, p.66
9. *Trioedd Ynys Prydein: The Triads of the Island of Britain*, p.15

Chapter 16: *Peredur the Son of Evrawc* (A tale from *The Mabinogion*)

1. Arrian, *Ars Tactica*, Chapter 34
2. https://archive.sacred-texts.com/neu/eng/vm/vmeng.htm
3. *Trioedd Ynys Prydein: The Triads of the Island of Britain*, p.234

Chapter 17: The Truth of the Grail

1. Stein, Walter Johanes (2018), 'King Arthur and the Problem of East and West', in *The Death of Merlin, Arthurian Myth and Alchemy*, Floris Books, p.125
2. 'King Arthur and the Problem of East and West', p.124
3. Guest, Lady Charlotte (1840), *The Mabinogion, Peredur the Son of Evrawc*, pp.109–10
4. *The Mabinogion, Peredur the Son of Evrawc*, p.122

Bibliography

Part I

Source material in the original and in translation

Rahn, Otto, *Crusade Against the Grail: The Struggle between the Cathars, the Templars, and the Church of Rome* (originally published in 1933 under the title *Kreuzzug gegen den Gral* by Urban Verlag), translated and annotated by Christopher Jones, published by Inner Traditions, Rochester, Vermot, 2006

Rahn, Otto, *The Court of Lucifer: A Voyage with Europe's Benevolent Ghosts* (originally published in 1937 under the title *Luzifers Hofgesind, eine Reise zu den guten Geistern Europas* by Schwarzhaupterverlag), later translated as *The Court of Lucifer: A Heretic's Journey in Search of the Light Bringers*, translated by Christopher Jones, published by Inner Traditions, Rochester, Dermot, 2008

Selected bibliography of secondary sources

Barraclough, David (2016), *Digging for Hitler, The Nazi Archaeologists Search for an Aryan Past*, Fonthill Media

Kirkpatrick, Sidney (2011), *Hitler's Holy Relics*, Simon & Schuster, London

O'Shea, Stephen (2000), *The Perfect Heresy, The Life and Death of the Cathars*, Profile Books, London

Padfield, Peter (2013), *Himmler Reichsführer-SS*, Thistle Publishing

Steigmann-Gall, Richard (2003), *The Holy Reich*, Cambridge University Press, New York

Waddell, L.A. (2014), *The British Edda*, Read Books

Selected internet sources

www.monsalvat.no/prelact1.htm

www.limelightmagazine.com.au/features/parsifal-richard-wagner-and-the-holy-grail/

www.wewelsburg.de/en/gedenkstaette-1933-1945/dauerausstellung.php

Part II

Source material in the original and in translation

Parzival, Wolfram von Eschenbach, translation with an introduction by Helen M. Mustard and Charles E. Passage, Vintage Books, New York, 1961

Peredur the Son of Evrawc, translated by Lady Charlotte Guest, www.ReadHowYouWant.com, Objective Systems Pty Ltd, 2006

Perceval, Chrétien de Troyes, translated by Ruth Harwood Cline, University of Georgia Press, 1985

Y Seint Greal, edited and translated by the Reverand Robert Williams MA in 1876, Jones Publishers, Gwynedd, 1987

Skene, William F., *The Four Ancient Books of Wales*, Edmonston and Douglas, Edinburgh, 1868

The High History of the Holy Grail (translated from *Perceval le Gallois ou le conte du Graal*, edited by M. Ch. Potvin in 1866 from MS 11145 Library of the Duke of Burgundy, Brussels), translated by Sebastian Evans (originally published 1903), Adventures Unlimited Press, 2016

Selected bibliography of secondary sources

Alcock, Lesley (2001), *Arthur's Britain*, Penguin, London

Ashley, Mike (2005), *King Arthur*, Robinson, London

Bromwich, Rachel (2014), *The Triads of the Island of Britain*, University of Wales Press, Cardiff

Hall, Richard (1996), *York*, Batsford, London

Mainman, Ailsa (2019), *Anglian York*, Blackthorn Press, Pickering

Morris, John (2004), *The Age of Arthur*, Phoenix, London

Ravenscroft, Trevor (1982), *The Cup of Destiny*, Samuel Weiser, USA

Sherman Loomis (1993), *Celtic Myth and Arthurian Romance* (first published by Columbia University Press, 1926), Constable, London

Smithett Lewis, Lionel (2004), St Joseph of Arimathea at Glastonbury (originally published by James Clarke and Co. Ltd, 1922), Lutterworth Press, Cambridge

Stein, Walter Johannes (2018), *The Death of Merlin* (originally published as articles 1924–36), Floris Books, Edinburgh

Tolstoy, Nikolai (1985), *The Quest for Merlin*, Little, Brown and Company, USA

Wood, Juliette (2012), *The Holy Grail*, University of Wales Press, Cardiff

Selected internet sources

www.bbc.co.uk/northyorkshire/iloveny/romans/2004/helen/index.shtml

Index